HOW TO BUILD A THRIVING

LAWN CARE

BUSINESS

SMART STRATEGIES TO ACHIEVE MAXIMUM PROFITS

PAUL JAMISON

Paul Jamison
Copyright © 2024 Paul Jamison

ISBN: 979-8-218-43784-8

www.ThePaulJamison.com

TABLE OF CONTENTS

DEDICATION

I dedicate this book to listeners of the Green Industry Podcast. I appreciate every listener who hangs out with Mr. Producer and myself in Podcast Land. I've had a lot of fun traveling to events, interviewing industry leaders, and doing my best to provide content that will help you grow your business and your profits. By listening to your struggles and pain points, I've been motivated to write this new book providing solutions. Thanks for listening to the podcast and I hope this book will help you tremendously.

INTRODUCTION

$928. THAT DAUNTING FIGURE WAS MY MOUNT Everest, a seemingly insurmountable peak in my financial landscape. It represented the rent I owed, a sum that, in my world, might as well have been a million dollars. Fresh out of college, reality hit me hard. Student loans, a borrowed car, and the necessities of life were my relentless creditors. But towering above them all was that $928 rent, a precipice on which my fragile financial stability teetered.

In that desperate phase of life, I was the embodiment of financial struggle, uncertainty and stress. My attempts at stability – selling Melaleuca vitamins, flipping Craigslist finds – were akin to putting a bandage on a gaping wound. Amidst this chaos, anxiety was my constant companion, an unwelcome shadow in my daily life.

Then came a spring day in Georgia, emblematic of change. As I embarked on a prayer walk, driven by a deep yearning for a breakthrough, my path led me to an unusual overgrown yard. That sight, set against a "For Sale" sign, sparked an unexpected turn in my journey. A call to the number on the sign, driven by curiosity, led to an impromptu lawn care job offer. There I was, without any equipment or experience, diving headfirst into the unknown for $60.

This was the unlikely inception of my lawn care journey, marked by borrowed equipment from my buddy Dave, a stubborn lawn mower, and a venture that initially set me back financially. Yet, from these humble beginnings, a relentless pursuit of improvement began, much like Tiger Woods returning to the practice range even after a triumphant Masters win. His dedication to constantly getting better, despite being at the pinnacle of his sport, resonates deeply with the pages of this book.

In the years that followed, my business was a relentless teacher. I navigated underpricing, hiring challenges, difficult customers, and operational inefficiencies. It was a chaotic, barely profitable venture, but a fertile ground for learning. Through this experience, I emerged with insights crucial not just for survival, but for thriving in business. I honed the art of pricing, understood the significance of choosing the right customers in the right neighborhoods, and streamlined billing and operations – the very lifeblood of a successful venture.

This book is my vessel to share these invaluable lessons with you. It's not solely a tale of turning around a struggling lawn care business; it's a guide for entrepreneurs at all stages – whether you're grappling with the chaos of a startup or seeking to elevate an already thriving business. This book offers insights for small business owners across various industries, from lawn care to painting, who aspire to refine their operations and edge closer to excellence.

My journey, encapsulated in this book, aligns with my mission of transforming lawn and landscape startups into thriving businesses. It's about moving from operational chaos to streamlined efficiency, achieving consistent profitability, and securing long-lasting financial success.

My goal is to guide you through the nuances of business optimization. Whether you're laying the foundation of your startup or seeking to outpace the competition, this book is a trove of insights and strategies to elevate your business.

Welcome to 'How to Grow Your Lawn Care Business.' Embark on this journey with me, and together, let's unlock the potential of your business, one page at a time."

CHAPTER 1

THE ENTREPRENEUR'S MINDSET

WELCOME TO THE JOURNEY OF TRANSFORMING your lawn care startup into a thriving, profitable business. If there's one thing I've learned in my years of navigating the lawn care industry, it's that success starts with the right mindset.

When I first embarked on this entrepreneurial path, I was equipped with nothing more than an employee's perspective, shaped by my experiences at jobs like Congress Lake Country Club (a local country club near my childhood home in Ohio) and Best Burger. These roles, while valuable in their own right, had instilled in me a mindset focused solely on the tasks at hand – a viewpoint that was soon to be challenged.

As Rabbi Daniel Lapin explains in "Thou Shall Prosper," being an employee is akin to being self-employed with just one customer: the company you work for. But stepping into the world of lawn care business ownership, I quickly realized that I was no longer playing a solo game. Instead, I was now responsible for satisfying a multitude of customers, each with their own set of expectations and demands.

This transition demanded a shift from just technical skills to a holistic view of business. It required understanding every angle, from equipment costs to labor, fuel, insurance, administrative expenses, and beyond. The challenge was no longer about just performing tasks; it was about managing risk, responsibility, and ensuring profitability.

One of my early realizations came when I charged $70 to spread pine straw – a sum that seemed substantial compared to my hourly wages in past jobs, but that price barely covered my business expenses. This moment was a wake-up call. I had to reevaluate my understanding of what my services were truly worth, moving beyond thinking in terms of hourly wages to understanding the overall profitability of my business.

My understanding of the entrepreneur's role grew as my business grew. I learned from others in the industry, like Kenny and Jamie, who shared their experiences and insights. Their stories helped me see the bigger picture – the importance of adapting to the ever-changing demands of running a business.

What kept me motivated during tough times was the freedom and satisfaction of being my own boss. Despite the challenges, the entrepreneurial path offered me control over my decisions and the direction of my business – a powerful motivator that drove me to continuously improve and grow.

Balancing a realistic understanding of my business's challenges with an optimistic outlook became crucial. It was about facing the facts, understanding the market, yet still having the hope and vision to push the business forward. Over the years, my approach to decision-making evolved significantly. I learned that tough decisions, whether letting go of difficult customers or making strategic operational changes, are an integral part of the entrepreneurial journey.

Your mindset as an entrepreneur directly impacts your leadership style and team dynamics. The standards you set, the attitude you bring, and the values you uphold are all reflected in your business's culture. Leading by example, with integrity and a commitment to excellence, is key to building a strong, successful team. This foundational mindset is what will guide us through the next phases of our journey.

In the chapters that follow, we will dive into the transformational stages of a lawn care business, starting with "Survival Mode Steve." This phase is where many of us begin – fighting to keep our heads above water, making ends meet, and learning from our myriad of mistakes. It's a critical period of growth, characterized by resilience and a determination to succeed against the odds.

From there, we will transition into "Growth Mode Greg," where the focus shifts from mere survival to expansion and scalability. We'll explore strategies for improving operations, investing in better equipment, and refining our financial management to support sustainable growth.

Finally, we will reach "Thriving Mode Tony," the pinnacle of our entrepreneurial journey. Here, success is not only measured by profitability but also by work-life balance, the quality of life it affords us and our teams, and the positive impact we have on our communities. "Thriving Mode Tony" symbolizes the ultimate goal: a business that not only survives but flourishes, allowing us to live our lives to the fullest.

As we embark on this journey together, remember that adopting the entrepreneurial mindset is not just about thinking differently; it's about acting differently. It's about taking responsibility for every aspect of your business and leading it toward success. Let's transform your lawn care business from one characterized by chaos to one now defined by efficiency and profit, navigating through the stages of "Survival Mode Steve," "Growth Mode Greg," and "Thriving Mode Tony," each step of the way.

CHAPTER 2

SURVIVAL MODE STEVE: OVERCOMING INITIAL CHALLENGES

T HE SPRING AND SUMMER OF 2011 marked the beginning of a journey that many entrepreneurs in the lawn care industry know all too well. It was a time when the excitement of starting my own business quickly collided with the reality of what it truly meant to run it. This was my "Survival Mode Steve" phase, a period characterized by significant challenges and the relentless pursuit to overcome them.

Cash flow was my most immediate and pressing challenge. As I gained new lawn customers, I soon realized that borrowing equipment was not a sustainable long-term solution. I needed my own gear, a realization that led to a series of staggered investments: first a string trimmer, then a lawn mower, and eventually, a used Ford F150. But as my equipment arsenal grew, so did my expenses. Repairs, fuel, job materials – these were not just unexpected costs but regular operational ones, something I hadn't fully anticipated.

My financial management was chaotic at best. I felt like a leaf caught in a rapid stream, being pulled along without control. I was digging myself into a financial hole, one that seemed increasingly difficult to climb out of. Besides the growing business expenses, I had my personal bills to pay, including rent and groceries. Paying part-time laborers added to the strain, as did the fuel costs of traveling across metro Atlanta to service clients in Lawrenceville, Johns Creek, Winder, and Duluth. I lacked route density, which meant more time and money spent on travel and less on actual profitable work.

Labor was another critical challenge. I needed help, especially for physically demanding tasks, but aligning schedules with part-time workers was a logistical nightmare. And when it came to pricing, I was severely undercharging for my services, a holdover from my employee mindset that failed to account for the true costs of running a lawn care business.

A particular experience that stands out from this period was an unexpected trip to Ohio for a funeral. Unlike the carefree travels of my youth, this journey was fraught with worry about my business back home. I had clients relying on me, and for the first time, I truly felt the weight of business ownership. It was a stark reminder of the level of commitment and planning required to sustain a business.

Slowly but surely, I started making changes. Upgrading equipment was a priority, not just for efficiency but also for professionalism. I also began focusing on building route density, which helped reduce operational costs and allowed me to serve my clients better. Perhaps the most important change was in my pricing strategy. I started to value my services correctly, ensuring they reflected the actual costs and effort involved.

For anyone starting out in the lawn care industry, my advice is to be mindful of your initial costs. Calculate them meticulously and ensure your prices not only cover these costs but also provide a margin for profit. Focus on building a client base in a concentrated area to maximize efficiency. Above all, prepare for the unexpected – sound financial management is key to navigating through this survival mode stage of the business.

The journey from "Survival Mode Steve" to "Growth Mode Greg," which I will explore in the next chapter, was marked by learning from these early challenges and laying the groundwork for a sustainable business. This initial phase, while tough, is a crucial period of learning and growth, where the foundations of a successful lawn care business are laid.

CHAPTER 3

FROM STRUGGLE TO STRATEGY: THE ROAD FROM SURVIVAL MODE STEVE TO GROWTH MODE GREG

EMBARKING ON THE JOURNEY FROM SURVIVAL Mode Steve to Growth Mode Greg was a transformative period in my lawn care business venture. It marked a significant shift from grappling with the teething problems of a newborn startup to laying the foundational stones for a sustainable and thriving business. This transition, while fraught with challenges, was also an era of profound learning and growth. It was during this time that I started to internalize the lessons of my early struggles and began to pivot towards a more strategic and structured approach to my business.

In those early years, my business was more of a scramble than a strategy. I was constantly trying to stay afloat, dealing with the aftermath of underpricing my services, wrestling with inefficient equipment, and spreading myself too thin across a disorganized client roster. However, it was this very state of chaos that propelled me to seek a better way, a path that would lead me out of the survival mindset and into a phase of genuine growth and development.

My turning point came during the quiet, reflective hours at my job as a radio station personality. In those moments of solitude, I found solace and guidance in the stories and experiences of other lawn care professionals who generously shared their journeys on YouTube. Channels like *Geek to Freak, Lawn Care Rookie, Keith Kalfas, Stanley Dirt Monkey Genadek, Johnny Mow*, and others became my nightly companions, offering insights and advice that began to reshape my understanding of the lawn care business.

Their videos were more than just entertainment; they were lifelines. They provided practical tips on everything from equipment selection to pricing strategies, but more importantly, they offered a glimpse into the potential of what my business could become. I was particularly inspired by Greg from Geek to Freak, whose journey from a struggling startup to a successful business owner mirrored the path I wanted to take. His success stories, along with the insights from others in the lawn care community, fueled my determination to evolve my business. I had hope again. I knew if Greg could do it, then I could too!

Emboldened by this newfound knowledge, I started implementing changes. I began optimizing my client list for route density, investing in better equipment, and most critically, revising my pricing strategy to reflect the true value of my services. It was a time of significant overhaul, requiring not just hard work but a complete shift in my business approach.

This period of transformation was challenging but deeply rewarding. I could see tangible improvements in my business—the once erratic cash flow began to stabilize, the quality of my services improved, and I found myself spending less time fixing mistakes and more time planning for the future.

The lessons I learned during this phase were invaluable. They taught me that success in the lawn care business requires more than just technical skills. It demands an understanding of the market, strategic pricing, effective marketing, and financial management. It's about creating a brand that resonates with your target customer and building a business that not only survives but thrives.

For those who are still navigating the early stages of your lawn care business, remember that this phase, while demanding, is foundational to your future success. Learn from the experiences of those who have tread this path before, utilize the resources available to you, and most importantly, keep believing in your ability to evolve your business.

As we progress through this book, I will delve deeper into the strategies and insights that helped me transition from Survival Mode Steve to Growth Mode Greg. It's a journey that encapsulates not just the growth of a business, but the growth of an entrepreneur. The road to becoming Thriving Tony, a symbol of success and satisfaction in the lawn care business, begins with these foundational steps. Let's continue this journey together, transforming challenges into opportunities for growth and success.

CHAPTER 4

THRIVING MODE TONY: CULTIVATING A BUSINESS AND LIFE IN FULL BLOOM

E MBARKING ON THE LAWN CARE BUSINESS journey is akin to nurturing a garden. It requires patience, effort, and the right strategies to see it flourish. In my journey, transitioning from Survival Mode Steve and Growth Mode Greg, I've come to realize that true success is not just about scaling up. It's about thriving – in business and life. Thriving Mode Tony represents not just a successful business but a life well-lived, where professional accomplishments and personal happiness coexist in harmony.

Tony Rudolph's story exemplifies this balance beautifully. Operating in Reynolds Plantation in Lake Oconee, Georgia, Tony's lawn care business is a testament to efficiency and profitability. He has mastered the art of route density, ensuring his operations are streamlined and his clients are all within a close-knit area. But what sets Tony apart is not just his business acumen; it's his commitment to his family and community. Despite his busy schedule, Tony ensures quality time with his family, actively participates in his local church, and is a respected figure in his community. His business thrives, but so do his relationships and personal life.

Jason Creel in Trussville, Alabama, mirrors Tony's path. With a focus on fertilizer and weed control, Jason has built a profitable business with remarkable efficiency. His success, however, is not confined to the realms of work. Jason is a family man, dedicated to his wife and children, ensuring his business commitments never overshadow his family responsibilities. His business thrives, but more importantly, so does his family life.

Scaling up can often lead to losing sight of what truly matters. Andy Mulder's story in Crown Point, Indiana, challenges this notion. Andy's landscaping business, generating substantial revenue through hardscaping and lawn maintenance, is a model of profitability. Yet, Andy remains deeply connected to the hands-on aspect of his work and his family. His weekends are dedicated to his children, and he enjoys life's pleasures, like vacations with his wife. Andy's business is not just thriving; it's a vehicle for a fulfilling life.

When we talk about thriving, it's not limited to owner-operated businesses. North Point Outdoors in New Hampshire demonstrates how larger operations can also embody the essence of Thriving Mode Tony. Despite being a multi-million-dollar enterprise, the company maintains a culture of respect, integrity, and balance. The success of North Point Outdoors is not just measured in revenue but in the quality of life it affords its team and the impact it has on the community.

Thriving Mode Tony is about creating a business that serves your life, not the other way around. It's about building an enterprise that reflects your values and supports your vision for life. Whether you're an owner-operator like Tony Rudolph or leading a larger team like North Point Outdoors, the principles remain the same: prioritize efficiency, nurture your team, value your customers, and never lose sight of your personal goals and relationships.

In the next chapter, I will share the strategies that have helped me and others achieve this balance. From smart pricing and effective marketing to team management and personal development, we will explore how to build a lawn care business that not only succeeds financially but also enriches your life and the lives of those around you. Join me on this journey of discovery, where we learn to cultivate not just a thriving business but a life in full bloom.

CHAPTER 5

FINANCIAL FUNDAMENTALS – MASTERING YOUR MONEY

I N MY JOURNEY FROM A FLEDGLING lawn care business owner to achieving financial stability, I've discovered that mastering financial fundamentals is as crucial as mastering the art of lawn care itself. It's akin to learning the basics of basketball—dribbling, shooting, and passing—before playing in a game. If you can grasp these financial basics, you're setting yourself up for success, not just in business, but in life.

My story intertwines with that of Allen Iverson, the basketball legend, whose financial downfall serves as a stark reminder of the importance of financial literacy. Despite earning over $200 million throughout his career, Iverson found himself in financial turmoil, eventually becoming my neighbor in a modest apartment complex. This was a jolting illustration of how, without budgeting and financial management, even the most substantial earnings can evaporate.

Allen Iverson's story isn't just a cautionary tale; it's a clear call for the necessity of living within our means, regardless of our income. It demonstrates that without a budget, it's alarmingly easy to spend everything we make—or more, leading to debt. This principle holds true whether you're making millions on the basketball court or running a lawn care business.

Budgeting, both in our personal lives and in our business, is the cornerstone of financial health. It's about planning where every dollar should go before the month even starts and then, critically, reviewing how you actually spent that money. This discipline is the key to widening the gap between income and expenses, which is the foundation of wealth building.

For instance, a realistic household budget might look something like this:

- Mortgage/Rent: $2,500
- Groceries: $600
- Utilities (Electricity, Water, Internet): $300
- Car Payment/Transportation: $400
- Insurance (Health, Auto): $500
- Savings/Investments: $600
- Entertainment/Miscellaneous: $300
- Total Monthly Income Required: $5,200

This example highlights the importance of allocating funds wisely and ensuring your lifestyle is sustainable based on your income. It's about making conscious decisions to avoid lifestyle creep and ensuring that you're not only living within your means but also saving and investing for the future. If you know that it takes $5,200 to operate your household, then in your lawn care business you need to make sure the business is earning enough so you can pay yourself at least $5,200 (or more, after taxes) as well as cover all the other expenses associated with the business and then some so you are profitable.

The principles of budgeting extend seamlessly into business finance. Understanding your business costs, pricing your services correctly, and managing cash flow are all underpinned by the discipline of budgeting. This chapter's focus on personal finance is intentional; mastering personal budgeting sets a solid foundation for handling your business finances effectively.

In the next chapter, we'll dive deeper into the financial operations of a lawn care business. We'll explore overhead cost recovery, pricing strategies, and how to read and understand financial statements like the profit and loss statement, balance sheet, and statement of cash flows. We'll also cover the critical aspect of saving for taxes to ensure your business not only survives but thrives.

Conclusion: A Path to Financial Prosperity

Remember, the journey to financial prosperity in your lawn care business starts with mastering the fundamentals of personal finance. Living below your means, budgeting meticulously, and planning for the future are practices that will serve you well in both your personal and business finances.

As we move forward, let's apply these principles to our businesses with the same discipline and intentionality. By doing so, we prepare ourselves not just for financial stability, but for the kind of prosperity that allows us to live a life rich in experiences, security, and fulfillment.

CHAPTER 6

MOW MONEY: FINANCIAL MANAGEMENT FOR THE THRIVING LAWN BUSINESS

ENSURING PROFITABILITY IN A LAWN CARE business requires a strategic approach to financial management. From comprehensively understanding your expenses to devising effective pricing strategies, every aspect plays a crucial role in building a sustainable and thriving business. This chapter delves into the essential financial components, offering a clear blueprint for lawn care entrepreneurs to secure their business's profitability.

Understanding Your Business Expenses

The first step to ensuring profitability is to have a detailed understanding of both your direct and indirect costs. It took me several years of experience and some really good bookkeepers to realize that there are a lot more expenses than we realize. Here's a breakdown of some of the most common expenses:

Direct Costs

- **Equipment:** Costs include initial purchases and ongoing maintenance for mowers, edgers, trimmers, blowers, etc... Maintenance encompasses oil changes, air and oil filter replacements, blade sharpening and more. Then keep in mind this equipment will eventually need repairs and the lawn mowers will need new blades, the string trimmers will need new string etc... This stuff all adds up fast and this is just the basic equipment and it gets more complex when you add bigger machinery such as mini skid steer or a regular skid steer, etc... and then you need larger trailers to haul the bigger equipment and so on and so on. As expensive as all the equipment is, typically that is not even the biggest expense. The biggest expense is usually the labor.

- **Labor:** Wages for your employees, including overtime, and payments to subcontractors for outsourced services like irrigation and lighting, grading, tree services, stump removal, design and installation, or any other services you sub out. It's hard to recruit team members to work in the elements. Mowing in the hot summer or blowing leaves in the chilly fall is not as attractive for laborers as working a nice air conditioning job. However, finding and keeping the right labor is essential to success in this industry. And if you want the best, we need to pay them accordingly, which can be expensive. We will talk about pricing in the next chapter, but we must make sure our prices are high enough so we can afford great reliable laborers.

- **Materials:** Expenses for sod, grass seeds, topsoil, fertilizers, mulch, pine straw, decorative rock, stones, plants, trees, seasonal flowers and other landscaping materials. And keep in mind the delivery fees for these materials and the dumping fees for jobs where you need to haul away debris.

- **Fuel:** Costs for operating lawnmowers, other equipment, and fuel for work vehicles. Or if you are going the route of battery equipment, there are the battery chargers and battery costs.

Indirect Costs

- **Insurance:** General liability, equipment protection, commercial vehicle insurance, and possibly more, depending on your specific business needs.

- **Marketing and Advertising:** Costs can range from vehicle signage to online advertising and traditional print media, just to name a few.

- **Office and Shop Expenses:** Rent and utilities for your storage units, office space, or both, depending on your business structure.

- **Software and Technology:** Monthly fees for CRM systems like Jobber and accounting software like QuickBooks Online. To start a free trial with Jobber visit getjobber.com/paul

- **Professional Services:** Payments for essential services such as bookkeeping and accounting. If you have listened to my podcast for any length of time you know I recommend a quality, reputable bookkeeper, accountant, tax preparer, and financial planner to make sure you are managing your business finances wisely.

- **Uniforms:** Expenses for purchasing, maintaining (including cleaning), and periodically replacing uniforms to ensure employees present a professional image and comply with safety standards. This includes shirts, hoodies, pants, safety vests, hats, and any other branded apparel.

These costs collectively form the financial backbone of your lawn care business. There can be other expenses as well, but these are the most common ones. Recognizing and accurately account-ing for them is vital for setting your service prices appropriately and making sure you have enough customers so your business is earning enough money for this business to be truly profitable.

Ensuring You're Paid:

One of the most overlooked aspects in the realm of lawn care business management is the owner's compensation. Many propri-etors often neglect to allocate themselves a fair, consistent salary that mirrors the significance and workload of their role. This over-sight isn't just a matter of personal finance; it's a crucial component of your business's pricing strategy and overall financial health. Your ability to draw a regular salary should be factored into your service pricing, guaranteeing that you can comfortably manage all business-related expenses, taxes, and your own compensation without endangering the company's profitability.

In a revealing conversation with Megan and Joey Coberly of The Landscaping Bookkeeper on my podcast, they pinpointed the primary fiscal oversight they've encountered after scrutinizing the accounts of numerous lawn care operations. The prevailing issue? A significant number of lawn care entrepreneurs fail to prioritize their own compensation adequately. This isn't about merely scraping by but ensuring that your business structure supports a healthy owner's salary. It's imperative to cultivate a robust customer base and establish pricing that accommodates comprehensive business costs—allowing not just for operational expenses and tax obliga-tions but for a rightful salary for you, the owner. This balanced approach to business finance underscores the importance of your role and contributes to a sustainable, profitable business model.

Tax Strategies and Planning

Keeping your personal and business finances separate simplifies tax planning and financial clarity. Allocate a portion of each transaction to a designated savings account for taxes, ensuring you're prepared for estimated tax payments. Regularly consulting with a professional can provide guidance on setting up an efficient payroll system and tax planning to keep your finances in order. There are no shortcuts here, Uncle Sam needs to be paid and it's our duty to be proactive to make sure that we are appropriately setting money aside so when the tax bills are due we have faithfully saved enough to pay the tax bills on time. I am not an expert in international tax law, but I do know that here in the United States of America if you get behind on taxes, the interest and penalties can be overwhelming. Again, I can't stress it enough, hire quality professionals who can be in your corner to help you understand your tax responsibilities and to keep you accountable to make sure you are setting aside the appropriate funds so you can pay all your tax bills on time and in full.

The Importance of Financial Statements

Regular review of your Profit and Loss Statement, Balance Sheet, and Cash Flow Statement is non-negotiable. These documents offer insights into your business's financial health, guiding informed decision-making:

- **Profit and Loss Statement:** Demonstrates profitability over a specific period by outlining revenues and expenses.

- **Balance Sheet:** Provides a snapshot of your financial standing at any given moment, detailing assets, liabilities, and equity.

- **Cash Flow Statement:** Tracks the flow of cash in and out, crucial for managing liquidity.

Conclusion: The Path to Profitability

Mastering the financial side of your lawn care business isn't just about the cash coming in; it's about strategically managing every penny to ensure your business not only grows but thrives sustainably. Accurate cost tracking and vigilant financial management are the keystones to turning a profit and securing a future for your business. The truth is, many of us in the lawn care industry excel at technical work. We can transform any lawn into a showcase of manicured excellence and take immense pride in our craftsmanship. Yet, delivering top-notch service is only one piece of the business success puzzle. Equally crucial is our prowess in financial management. Understanding how to interpret and act on the information in our financial statements is critical. But remember, you're not in this alone. Building a robust financial team—comprising of a knowledgeable bookkeeper, a diligent tax preparer, and a savvy financial advisor—is key. Their expertise can help you navigate the complexities of financial management, ensuring your business remains profitable, taxes are paid promptly, and your investments are growing, harnessing the power of compound interest. Stay engaged and proactive in conversations with your financial team. Their insights will guide you toward wise financial decisions, laying a solid foundation for wealth accumulation and the long-term success of your lawn care venture.

CHAPTER 7

PRICING MASTERY: STRATEGIES FOR LAWN CARE SUCCESS

I N THE REALM OF LAWN CARE, success hinges not just on the quality of your service but also on mastering the art of pricing. Of course, you also need the right quantity of customers in the proper service area, but we will cover that later when we discuss the best ways to market your business. For now, let's dive deeper into pricing your services. Getting your pricing right from the onset is crucial. It's the difference between thriving in business or finding yourself hustling on the side just to make ends meet, as I once did balancing lawn care with evenings serving Fettuccine Alfredo at Carrabba's. This chapter delves into the practicalities of pricing your services appropriately—ensuring you cover your expenses, pay yourself a deserving salary, meet tax obligations, remain profitable, and have funds to reinvest in your business's growth.

One of the most common mistakes that lawn and landscaping business owners make is simply not charging enough. As I mentioned in chapter one, if we still have an employee mindset that can be dangerous when we go to price our services because in all likelihood we won't fully calculate how much it really costs to run our business and therefore our prices won't be high enough to sustain our business. It doesn't help that "Chuck in the Truck" and the neighborhood kid are mowing for so cheap, that you can't compete with their prices. Let's explore the three main pricing models and consider their applicability in the lawn care industry:

Cost-Plus Pricing: This model involves calculating the total cost of providing a service—accounting for both direct and indirect expenses—then adding a markup to ensure a profit. It's straightforward and ensures costs are covered, but the challenge lies in determining a markup that keeps you competitive yet profitable.

Value-Based Pricing: Adopting a value-based pricing strategy means you set your prices based on what your customers believe your service is worth, rather than simply covering your costs. This method demands a thorough understanding of your clients' needs and how they view the distinct advantages your lawn care brings. It's a powerful way to boost your earnings, especially for services that stand out or when your business has built a reputable brand. Take, for instance, certain upscale gated communities in Atlanta, home to lavish million-dollar estates. The homeowners in these areas aren't looking for just any lawn service; they seek out professionals who can provide exceptional care, making their lawns look immaculate. My buddy in Atlanta has carved out a niche for himself with "reel" mowing services, cutting grass to the precise, low height you'd see on a golf course fairway. Despite the property sizes being comparable to others in the vicinity, he can command a higher price due to this specialized offering. His use of finely honed reel mowers ensures a superior cut, leaving lawns looking as prestigious as the greens at "Augusta National." This example underscores how tailoring your services to meet specific customer desires and delivering unparalleled quality can justify premium pricing and significantly increase your profitability.

Competitive Pricing: Here, your pricing is informed by what competitors in your market are charging for similar services. It's vital to strike a balance between being competitively priced and ensuring your rates cover costs and achieve profitability. Again with this approach, you want to compare the prices of the companies who are professional, who have been around for a long time, have a ton of positive Google reviews, and have a high revenue. DO NOT compare or worry about what the neighborhood kid is charging or Chuck in the Truck.

Each model has its place, depending on your business goals, the services you offer, and the market you operate in. Cost-plus pricing ensures your expenses are covered, value-based pricing capitalizes on the unique benefits you offer, and competitive pricing helps you stay relevant in your market. The key is to blend insights from each model to develop a pricing strategy that works for your lawn care business.

Conducting Market Research

Conducting thorough market research is a cornerstone for setting up your lawn care business for success. It equips you with the necessary insights to price your services competitively, ensuring you're in line with industry standards while also carving out your unique value proposition. Here's how to dig deeper into market research to make informed pricing decisions.

Take the time to study what other lawn care businesses in your area are offering and at what price points. This doesn't mean a superficial glance but a deep dive into their service packages, pricing strategies, and how they communicate their value to customers. A simple way to start is by exploring the websites of leading landscaping companies in your region. For instance, when exploring a top company's site in the Atlanta area, you might find detailed descriptions of their service packages. While you might need to enter an address to get specific pricing, understanding the structure of their offerings gives you a framework for how services can be bundled and presented.

But don't stop at online research. Engaging with local nurseries and suppliers can provide invaluable insights. These establishments are not just points of purchase but hubs of community knowledge within the landscaping industry. By fostering relationships with the staff and owners, you gain access to a wealth of information. Queries about the going rates for specific services like mulch installation per yard, pine straw bale installation, or plant installation prices can yield surprisingly detailed responses.

For those new to the lawn care industry, this information is gold. If you're still building your business and don't have a detailed record of past financials to determine your costs accurately, aligning your prices with those of the established "Big Boys" in the market can be a strategic move. It positions you competitively while you work on fine-tuning your understanding of your business's unique expenses.

Remember, market research is not a one-time task but an ongoing process. The landscaping industry is dynamic, with prices fluctuating due to various factors such as seasonal demand, supply chain changes, and evolving customer preferences. Keeping your finger on the pulse of the market means you can adjust your pricing strategy as needed, ensuring you remain competitive while also covering your costs and achieving a healthy profit margin.

In summary, market research for your lawn care business involves a balanced approach of online investigation, direct engagement with local industry participants, and continuous monitoring of market trends. This approach not only helps you set competitive prices but also informs the development of service packages that meet the needs and expectations of your target customers, setting the stage for a successful and profitable lawn care business.

Setting Your Prices

With a firm grasp of your costs and a clear understanding of the market, you're ready to set your prices. Here's how to approach it:

- Calculate Your Costs: Include all direct and indirect expenses. Knowing your breakeven point is crucial. If you need help with this check out our resources at greenindustrypodcast. com which can help you determine your breakeven man hour rate.

- Assess the Market: Use your market research to understand the going rates for services you offer. Remember only research companies who have been around a while and are larger. They have figured out how to cover their costs.

- Consider Your Value Proposition: If you offer unique benefits or superior service, don't be afraid to price accordingly. For example, I have a friend who only offers reel mowing. And he charges a premium price to create that golf course-type look for his customers.

- Be Strategic with Service Packages: Offer tiered packages to cater to different customer needs and budgets. This not only provides options for your customers but also opportunities for upselling.

- Stay Flexible and Responsive: The market and your costs will evolve. Regularly review and adjust your prices to reflect these changes.

Incorporating these strategies into your pricing approach will not only cover your costs and secure profitability but also position your lawn care business for sustainable growth and success.

Pricing for Growth

Remember, pricing is not just about covering costs and earning a profit; it's also a strategic tool for business growth. By understanding and implementing effective pricing strategies, you lay the foundation for a thriving lawn care business that can adapt to market changes, satisfy customers, and outperform competitors.

This chapter has laid the foundation for effective pricing strategies in your lawn care business, setting the stage for enduring success and growth. By adopting these tailored approaches, you're not just ensuring your business's survival; you're propelling it towards prosperity and a competitive edge in the market. The rewards of meticulous pricing are substantial, offering financial stability and the opportunity for expansion. As we transition to the next chapter, we'll delve into the nuances of billing—structuring and securing payments for your services—ensuring that your financial operations are as streamlined and efficient as your pricing strategy. For a complimentary guide on how to price your services effectively, please visit my website at ThePaulJamison.com.

CHAPTER 8

GETTING PAID RIGHT – BILLING TIPS FOR YOUR LAWN CARE BUSINESS

RUNNING A LAWN CARE BUSINESS MEANS you've got to be sharp about how you get paid. Imagine you're running a lemonade stand. You wouldn't want to wait weeks to get paid for a cup of lemonade, right? Well, it's the same with mowing lawns or doing fertilizer and weed control (aka fert and squirt). You do the work, and you should get paid on time, so you can keep your business running smoothly.

Why Billing Matters So Much

Let's talk about billing – that's just a fancy word for sending out a bill and making sure you get paid. Doing this right helps your cash keep flowing, so you don't end up scratching your head, wondering where your money went. If you're not careful, you might end up like a juggler with too many balls in the air, and that's a sure way to drop them all.

In earlier chapters, we uncovered just how many costs you've got to cover in a lawn care biz. It is a lot, right? From all the equipment you need to the employees, you have pay to help you out. And let's not forget about setting aside money for taxes and paying yourself for all your hard work. That's why you've got to price your services smartly – to cover all these expenses and still have some money left over for yourself. But, while mastering your prices is crucial, so is how and when you get paid.

The Smart Way to Bill

Years ago, I learned something cool from Jonathan Pototschnik who runs a big lawn care company. He had a rule: No cash, no checks, just cards on file. That means before you even start working for a customer, you've got their payment info saved, so getting paid is a breeze.

This method is gold, especially for regular lawn care work like mowing, edging, and blowing leaves. You want to set things up so you're not waiting forever to get your money. If you do big projects, like redoing someone's entire backyard, getting a check is okay since those jobs can cost a lot more.

When to Charge Your Customers

Now, how often should you charge your customers? In places like Atlanta, where I'm from, the big lawn care companies charge a flat fee every month, all year round. This makes sure the cash keeps coming in, even in the slower months. But if you live somewhere with a real winter, you might charge only for the months you're actually working.

The key is to get paid before or right when you do the work. Charging the day of service is one way to do it. Or, charge a flat monthly fee, so you know exactly how much you're getting each month. This helps avoid any surprises with your cash flow.

Switching to a Better Billing System

What if you're stuck in the old way of doing things – waiting until after the work is done to send a bill and then waiting some more to get paid? It's time for a change. Talk to your customers. Let them know you're updating how you do billing for the better. Most folks will understand, especially when you explain it's all about providing them with the best service possible.

A Few Tips for Bigger Landscaping Jobs

For big jobs, like installing sod or doing a landscaping makeover, you might ask for part of the payment upfront, another part when you start, and the final payment when you're done. This way, you're not doing a ton of work without seeing any of the money. But first, check with your governing rules and regulations on this. Some states here in the United States of America have rules about how you can collect your draws. If you have the freedom to do it whatever way you want, then I would go with the ⅓ deposit to get on the schedule, ⅓ the day you physically get started on the job, and then the final ⅓ the day you complete the job before you leave the customers property. I like to make sure the customer is home when we are just about done, so when the job is completed you can walk the property with the customer, making sure they are thrilled with the result of your work. Then before you leave the property collect the final ⅓ payment.

The Bottom Line

Getting your billing right is like having the right tools to do the job. It makes everything smoother and keeps your business healthy. Remember, the goal is to make sure you can pay for everything your business needs, pay yourself, save for taxes, and still have money left over to grow your business. With the right approach to billing, you're setting yourself up for success. You still have to budget and manage all the money coming in appropriately. But, just don't make the mistake of customers owing you money or delayed payments. Be proactive by getting customers' cards on file and having your billing policies in place and adhered to so that you are getting paid on time.

CHAPTER 9

FINDING YOUR IDEAL CUSTOMERS

IN THE DYNAMIC WORLD OF LAWN care business, understanding your numbers and setting appropriate service pricing forms the bedrock of your venture's financial health. However, the lifeblood that sustains its vitality and growth is your clientele. Not just any customers, but the *ideal* ones—those who appreciate the value of your service, align with your business ethos, and contribute to your profitability. This chapter delves into the art and science of attracting the right customers to your lawn care business. I've made the mistake of having too many PITA (pain in the a**) customers and will teach you how to avoid that.

Knowing Your Area: Identifying Your Ideal Customer

The journey to attracting your ideal customers begins with a deep dive into understanding who they really are. This involves constructing a detailed profile based on demographic, geographic, psychographic, and behavioral factors.

Imagine you're a farmer selecting seeds; you'd choose those best suited to your land's conditions. Similarly, identifying your ideal customer involves understanding not just the "what" but the "who" you're catering to. For instance, my exploration into this process unveiled a particular demographic: women aged 45-65, typically married with children, residing in the suburban country clubs, where the household income comfortably exceeds $200,000.

Such detailed profiling is instrumental. It guides where and how you'll sow your marketing efforts, ensuring they fall on fertile ground—a place where your business's values and your customers' needs align perfectly.

Here are some questions to consider when building your dream customer profile:

Demographic Information:

- What is the age range of my ideal customer?
- What is their gender?
- What is their marital or family status (e.g., single, married, families with young children)?
- What is their income level?
- What is their occupation or profession?

Geographic Location:

- Where do my ideal customers live?
- Are they in urban, suburban, or rural areas?
- Are there specific neighborhoods or regions where my services are most needed?

Lifestyle and Interests:

- What hobbies or interests do they have?
- How do they spend their free time?
- What values are important to them (e.g., sustainability, community involvement)?

Property Characteristics:

- What type of property do they own (e.g., residential homes, commercial properties, rental properties)?
- What is the size of their property?
- Are there common features in their properties that require specialized care (e.g., large lawns, ornamental gardens, hardscaping)?

Service Needs and Preferences:

- What specific lawn care services are they looking for (e.g., basic lawn maintenance, landscaping design, specialty treatments)?
- How frequently do they require these services?
- What are their priorities when choosing a lawn care provider (e.g., price, quality, eco-friendliness)?

Pain Points and Challenges:

- What challenges do they face in maintaining their lawn or garden?
- Have they had bad experiences with lawn care providers in the past?
- What are their biggest frustrations with their current lawn or garden?

Decision-Making Process:

- Who makes the decision to hire a lawn care service in the household or business?
- What factors influence their decision-making process?
- How do they prefer to be contacted and communicated with?

Communication and Marketing Preferences:

- Where do they look for information on lawn care services (e.g., online search, social media, word of mouth)?
- What type of marketing messages are they most responsive to?
- Do they follow brands or businesses on social media?

If you are listening to the audiobook I want to encourage you to pick up a copy of the paperback book on Amazon so you can fill out the following worksheet that is an ideal customer Profile.

IDEAL CUSTOMER PROFILE WORKSHEET

Demographic Information:

What is the age range of my ideal customer?

What is their gender?

What is their marital or family status (e.g., single, married, families with young children)?

What is their income level?

What is their occupation or profession?

Geographic Location:

Where do my ideal customers live?

Are they in urban, suburban, or rural areas?

Are there specific neighborhoods or regions where my services are most needed?

Neighborhood 1:

Neighborhood 2:

Neighborhood 3:

Lifestyle and Interests:

What hobbies or interests do they have?

How do they spend their free time?

What values are important to them (e.g., sustainability, community involvement)?

Property Characteristics:

What type of property do they own (e.g., residential homes, commercial properties, rental properties)?

What is the size of their property?

Are there common features in their properties that require specialized care (e.g., large lawns, ornamental gardens, hardscaping)?

Service Needs and Preferences:

What specific lawn care services are they looking for (e.g., basic lawn maintenance, landscaping design, specialty treatments)?

How frequently do they require these services?

What are their priorities when choosing a lawn care provider (e.g., price, quality, eco-friendliness)?

Pain Points and Challenges:

What challenges do they face in maintaining their lawn or landscape?

Have they had bad experiences with lawn care providers in the past?

What are their biggest frustrations with their current yard?

Decision-Making Process:

Who makes the decision to hire a lawn care service in the household or business?

What factors influence their decision-making process?

How do they prefer to be contacted and communicated with?

Communication and Marketing Preferences:

Where do they look for information on lawn care services (e.g., online search, social media, word of mouth)?

What type of marketing messages are they most responsive to?

Do they follow brands or businesses on social media?

I highly encourage you to thoroughly answer these questions. The more detail you can give to your dream customer the better. This will help you dial in your marketing efforts because you know exactly who you want to be your customer.

Cultivating Connections: Marketing Strategies That Resonate

With the ideal customer profile in hand, the next step is to employ a blend of traditional and digital marketing strategies to reach them effectively. The modern lawn care business thrives not just on the quality of service but equally on the quality of its connections with potential clients.

Traditional Marketing still holds sway in establishing local brand presence. Flyers, door hangers, and direct mail, particularly Every Door Direct Mail (EDDM), offer tangible touchpoints. On the Green Industry Podcast, over the years I've interviewed hundreds of lawn care business owners and from my research door hangers are the most effective traditional marketing tool. Digital marketing should certainly be apart of your overall marketing plan, but do not neglect traditional marketing. It still works in the home service industry.

Next, let's take a glance at digital marketing. The best practices for digital marketing is a well-crafted website, active social media engagement, and a robust Google Business Profile. These platforms ensure your business remains visible and attractive to your ideal clientele in the digital realm. Now, I am writing this book in the year 2024. Perhaps you are reading this years down the road and the digital marketing landscape may have shifted a bit, but for now these seem to be the best places to be. And it's not a la cart where you just select one, I would recommend being everywhere. For example, if I were to start a lawn care business today from scratch, after creating my ideal customer profile, I would then hit those neighborhoods with door hangers, I would also run facebook micro-targeted ads in those neighborhoods, while also making sure my Google Business Profile was attractive, have my Facebook Page and Instagram Page looking fresh and clean and of course having an excellent website. You want to do them all. But, let's take a deeper look into what a good website actually looks like.

A good website serves as the digital storefront of your lawn care business, offering a first impression that can either attract or repel potential clients. It should be professionally designed, reflecting the quality and reliability of the services you provide. Key components include:

- **Clear Branding:** Your logo, color scheme, and brand message should be prominently displayed, offering instant recognition and a professional appearance.

- **Easy Navigation:** Users should find what they need without hassle. A simple, intuitive layout ensures they can explore services, contact information, and booking options effortlessly.

- **Quality Content:** High-resolution images of your work, detailed descriptions of your services, and customer testimonials showcase your expertise and the results you deliver. And let me emphasize **your work!** I do coaching calls helping lawn care business owners grow their business and when onboarding a new coaching client I first take a look at their website and Google Business Profile. Over the years I just chuckle because I see the same stock photos. Please do not use any stock photos on your website. Have fresh pictures of your work and your team. Take the time to make these photos look good so you can represent yourself well to your potential dream customers.

- **Responsive Design:** With more people using mobile devices to browse the web, your site must look great and function well on screens of all sizes.

- **Contact Information:** Make it easy for clients to reach out by including your phone number, email address, and a contact form prominently on the site.

- **Call to Action (CTA):** Encourage visitors to take the next step, whether it's requesting a quote, booking a service, or calling for more information, with clear, compelling CTAs. The call to action buttons should be all over your website and very easy for website visitors to recognize and click on. This is the goal of the website to get them to click on that Call to Action button.

- **SEO Optimization:** Incorporate relevant keywords naturally into your content to improve your site's visibility on search engine results pages, drawing in more organic traffic.

- **Educational Resources:** Offering blog posts or articles about lawn care tips, seasonal maintenance advice, and other relevant topics can position you as an authority in your field, building trust with potential clients.

- **Social Media Links:** Integrate your social media profiles to extend the conversation and community building beyond your website. If your ideal customer is a residential customer, they more than likely are on Facebook and Instagram. If the ideal customer is a commercial client, they are more than likely on LinkedIn. If you need more help understanding social media strategy tune into my podcast, the Green Industry Podcast, I am continuously sharing the latest social media trends and tips with my listeners on the podcast.

- **Security Features:** Ensure your website is secure, especially if handling customer information or online transactions, to build trust and comply with regulations.

Now, that may be overwhelming if you are thinking how do I build a website that integrates all those suggestions. The good news is I found a company down in Pensacola, Florida that creates a banger website. They are called Footbridge Media and do phenomenal work. If you visit my website at greenindustrypodcast.com you can get a special deal with Footbridge Media. Make sure to tell them Paul Jamison sent you and they will give you a big discount and take good care of you, designing your website professionally and implementing all the suggestions I previously wrote about in this chapter.

I know that was a lot about what to include on your website, but many of those same principles carry over to your Google Business Profile. Typically, a person seeking lawn services is going to either ask their network of neighbors, friends or family who they recommend or they are going to go on the internet and type in "lawn care services near me" or something to that effect. And this is a golden opportunity for your Google Business Profile to appear. So what should your Google Business Profile include?

In my opinion the Google Business Profile is equally or even more important than your website. The reason is, in some cases this is going to be the first thing your potential dream customer sees. And this is our opportunity to connect and show them that we have the answer to their problem. First and foremost, your Google Business Profile should include real customer reviews and testimonials. In our day and age customer reviews carry a lot of weight. For example, just this past week I was searching for an app that has a golf tracer. Essentially, it will draw the path of the ball after you hit it. I just typed in golf ball tracer app. When I clicked on one, I immediately went to the reviews. And lo and behold the first one I clicked on only had 1 review! Although it was a 5 star review, I bounced quickly. By only having one review, it lacked enough credibility for me to download the app. I share my story to emphasize on your Google Business Profile you want quantity of reviews as well as quality (5 stars). I would get in the healthy habit of asking your happy customers to leave you a Google review. This should certainly be a standard operating procedure (SOP). Train your team after any enhancement job (sod install, grading job, tree service, flower install, mulch job etc...) that once you are done with the work to ask the customer to leave you a Google Review. You need to be proactive and intentional to ask because beefing up these Google Reviews is of the utmost importance to building your online credibiltiy. Now, if you are starting your Google Business Profile from scratch, I recommend reaching out to your happiest customers and asking them for a favor, kindly request they leave you a google review and emphasize to them how much you would appreciate that. In addition to a strong showing of customer reviews, make sure your Google Business Profile also has plenty of fresh pictures of your work and your team and please make sure that all your company's info appears accurate on your Google Business Profile.

I hope I didn't beat the dead horse with the Google Business Profile and website, but they are so important and I want to make sure you have a great website and Google Business Profile for your company. Next let's discuss building your brand identity and visual harmony. The visual and experiential essence of your brand is pivotal in setting you apart. Professional attire and vehicles emblazoned with your logo do more than just catch the eye; they weave the fabric of a cohesive and memorable brand experience. Consistency is key, enabling your brand to echo in the minds of your target audience. Reflecting on my discussions on the Green Industry Podcast, for selecting a distinctive color scheme you can draw inspiration from the vibrant palettes of NFL teams as seen on nfl.com. A harmonious contrast, such as the Pittsburgh Steelers' black and yellow or the Dallas Cowboys' silver and blue, or Green Bay Packers green and yellow can significantly elevate your brand's visual appeal. With 32 teams showcasing unique color combinations, there's ample inspiration to help crystallize your brand's visual identity. Yet, establishing a brand extends beyond color choices. Investing in a professionally designed logo and a signature company font ensures that every aspect of your branding, from vehicle wraps and website design to uniform aesthetics, speaks the same visual language. Utilize consistent hex codes for your colors across all marketing materials to maintain visual integrity, ensuring your brand appears polished and professional across every touchpoint.

Cultivating Client Connections: Making Your Lawn Care Business Unforgettable

In an era where your ideal customers are bombarded with options, engaging them effectively is the key to cultivating lasting loyalty. Dr. Frank Holleman, a regular contributor to the Green Industry Podcast, emphasizes the importance of omnipresence in today's marketing landscape. In the past, radio and newspapers were the mainstays of marketing, requiring around seven touchpoints to influence consumer behavior. Fast forward to today, and that number has jumped to approximately 21 touchpoints, thanks to the digital explosion.

Your ideal customers are likely scrolling through their social media feeds daily, making platforms like Facebook and Instagram prime real estate for your marketing efforts. It's essential to ensure your presence is not only seen but felt on these platforms. By actively engaging on social media, you provide a window into the quality and value of your services, directly into the lives of suburban families who value their home's curb appeal.

Leverage Instagram and Facebook not just as showcases but as interactive stages. Utilize Reels to share quick, captivating clips of your team in action, paired with trending sounds that highlight your meticulous work. Before-and-after photos are compelling evidence of your expertise, drawing viewers into a visual journey of transformation. Aim for daily posts to satisfy the algorithms and boost your visibility, but at the very least, maintain a consistent posting schedule.

Remember, a business-specific Facebook Page and Instagram account are vital to separating your professional presence from your personal life. For businesses targeting the commercial sector, a robust LinkedIn profile can also be a powerful tool in your marketing arsenal. Through strategic engagement and a well-crafted online presence, your lawn care business can stand out in a crowded market, turning casual browsers into loyal customers.

The Harvest:
A Thriving Lawn Care Business

Attracting your ideal customers isn't a one-time effort but a continuous process of nurturing and growth. It's about understanding deeply who your ideal customers are, reaching them through a mix of strategic marketing efforts, and continuously engaging them in ways that foster loyalty and advocacy.

The success of your lawn care business is deeply rooted in the quality of customers you attract and retain. By focusing on cultivating relationships with your ideal customers, you set the stage for sustainable growth and enduring success.

CHAPTER 10

MAKING YOUR LAWN CARE BUSINESS WORK EASIER AND FASTER

RUNNING A LAWN CARE BUSINESS MEANS you're always looking for ways to do your work quicker, without spending too much money, and still doing a great job. Think of it like playing a video game where you need to find the best shortcuts to win without running out of resources. In this chapter, we're going to talk about how you can make your lawn care business run smoother, just like finding the best paths in a game.

Why Making Things Easier Matters

Imagine if you had a map that showed you the quickest way to get from one lawn to the next. You'd save so much time and gas, right? That's what we want to achieve in your business. Making things easier means you can do more work without getting super tired or spending all your money on gas or windshield time. Windshield time is when you and your employees are just sitting in the truck commuting around town. Although its inevitable you do need to spend some time in your work vehicle driving from the shop to your customers properties, you want to minimize this time and be out on your customers property serving them and earning revenue.

Finding the Best Paths: Route Optimization

The first step to making things easier is planning your day so you're not driving all over town. You want to visit lawns that are close to each other on the same day. This way, you spend less time driving and more time mowing. I don't want to beat the dead horse on this point, but I have done way too many coaching calls trying to fix this problem. Just last month I was helping a coaching client of mine. A while back he picked up a really good commercial property about an hour and a half drive hours from his shop. He needed the money so he took the job. Long story short over the years he accumulated more properties surrounding that one. Now he spends a full day in that area and requires a crew of 3. It's 1.5 hours to drive there and 1.5 hours driving back. That's 3 hours in the truck each week going to that area. Keep in mind there are 3 men in the truck, 3 laborers x 3 hours of windshield times = 9 precious hours. After running some basic math I convinced him to move on from that area and invest those 9 man hours in the area near his shop where he should be dominating. He's going to finish out this season and the contract then move on. The point in sharing this story though is that with proper planning and clarity of your service area and sticking to those boundaries this could all be avoided. Here are some tips on how to improve and increase efficiency with your routes:

- **Use a Map App:** There are cool apps on the computer or your phone that help you find the best way to go to all your lawns with the least driving. It's like a game where you try to find the shortest path to save time and win!

- **Pick Customers Close Together:** Try to get customers who live near each other. It's like picking levels in a game that are close, so you don't waste time getting to the next one. If you are newer in the lawn care business and don't have a full roster of customers yet, then I would drop a pin in the neighborhood you want to dominate and try to build your business out from that area. Please keep in mind where your home is and where your shop or storage unit is.

Again our goal is not to be driving around town, but to be on customers' properties earning revenue.

- **Be Smart with Your Schedule:** Sometimes, you can choose which days you go to which lawns. Group them by where they are so you can do a bunch in the same area each day.

Planning Your Work Day: Job Scheduling

Next, we need to talk about making a good plan for each day. You want to make sure you're not just working hard, but working smart. That means doing your lawns in an order that makes sense and keeps your customers happy.

- **Customers' Wishes vs. Your Plan:** You want to listen to when your customers want their lawns done but also keep your driving short. Sometimes you can teach your customers why it's better to do their lawn on a day when you're already in their area. From my experiences most customers desire their maintenance done on a Thursday or Friday so it looks fresh and clean for the weekend. However, I don't like to guarantee what day I will be there for a customer. I simply tell them if they hire us we will have their property looking pristine year round, therefore they do not need to be concerned about what day we will be there.

- **Busy Seasons and Slow Times:** Know when you'll be super busy and when things are slow. Use the quiet times to get your tools ready and take a little break, so you're all set when it gets busy again. Rain days are often gifts from above. They can be great days to go to the shop and clean things up, repair equipment, get caught up on office work, etc...

- **Have a Plan for Surprises:** Sometimes, you'll get a last-minute call for a job. Have some open spots in your schedule for these surprises so you can fit them in without messing up your other plans. Also, rain is not a surprise. Unless you live in San Diego or a climate where it seldom rains, it's going to rain. Therefore, you need to have some margin in your schedule. If you do a lot of maintenance make sure you keep a day or two open at the end of the week in case of rain. For example, you may want to consider scheduling maintenance work (mow, edge, trim, blow) Monday-Thursday and keeping Friday open as a make up day for when it rains or other surprises come up. Whether it rains, or an employee doesn't show up or you have issues with equipment or your vehicle, you can easily get behind so keeping some scheduled time open to make up work is wise. Also, keep in mind that if you want to get involved in enhancement work such as installing plants, flowers, trees, sod, mulch, pine straw etc... you need to have that built into your schedule. Most of your maintenance customers are going to have these needs so you need to have a plan on when you will be able to perform these services if you choose to do so.

Taking Care of Your Tools

Your mowers, tools, vehicles, trailers etc. are like your game controllers – you can't play without them! Keeping them working well is super important. Now, some people justify buying everything brand new so there are less repairs, but that could be detrimental if you can't afford it. But for what your budget allows, take great care of what you do have.

- **Regular Check-ups:** Just like you need to eat right and exercise to stay healthy, your equipment needs regular check-ups to keep working great.

- **Keep Track of Your Tools:** Know when it's time to give your tools a little TLC. You can use a computer program or app to remind you when it's time for maintenance. Or you can do things the old fashioned way like Caleb Auman. He literally just uses a Sharpie marker and will write on this equipment like a skid steer when he does an oil change. The point is you should be organized and know when maintenance is due on your vehicles and equipment to avoid things breaking or not working pre-maturely.

- **Teach Your Team:** As you get new employees working for you, make sure they know how to use and take care of the tools properly. This way, they won't break them by accident. One summer I hired a gentleman, and I assumed he understood the big red gas can that says 50:1 mix all over it was to only be used in the power equipment. And the other gas can that was blue that says "Gas Only" was to be used for the lawn mowers. Well he carelessly poured the straight gas into the backpack blower and it completely ruined it. At the end of the day the blame was on me. I should have done better training to make sure he was fully aware of the difference of a 50:1 mix of oil and gas for the power equipment versus the regular gas for the mowers and trucks.

At heart I am a podcaster so you know I like my lists! Here are my Top 10 mistakes to avoid with maintaining your lawn equipment. Now please keep in mind I am not as mechanically gifted as my friend John Pajak aka the Gravel Back Mechanic. And the list can be much much longer than this, but from my experiences these are the bare bone essentials to pay close attention to when taking care of your company so that your tools are working as efficiently as possible.

Top 10 Mistakes to Avoid:

1. **Skipping Regular Maintenance Checks:**
   Neglecting routine inspections and maintenance can lead to bigger problems down the line. Blades get dull, engines lose efficiency, and minor issues can turn into major repairs. Plan regular maintenance.

2. **Ignoring Cleanliness:**
   Failing to clean equipment after use can cause a buildup of grass clippings, dirt, and debris. This not only affects performance but can also lead to rust and corrosion, shortening the equipment's lifespan. If you are not following Mitchell Gordy from Mithgo Outdoor Services on Instagram you should. His high standard for cleanliness is inspiring. I've been to his shop multiple times and his tools, mowers, tractor, vehicles, trailers are in tip top shape and that's because after each use it gets cleaned.

3. **Not Sharpening Blades Regularly:**
   Dull blades tear rather than cut grass cleanly, resulting in a poor finish and potentially harming the lawn. Regular sharpening ensures clean cuts and healthier grass. I would get in the routine of starting every morning off with fresh blades. There are various techniques to sharpen blades, but select a process that works best for you to sharpen your blades. Then after your done mowing each day, swap out the blades for some fresh razor sharp ones so when you start mowing the next morning you always start the day with fresh clean blades. This will create the best results and help you keep your customers happy they hired you and not Chuck in the Truck.

4. **Overlooking Air Filter Maintenance:**
Air filters clogged with dust and debris can reduce engine efficiency and increase fuel consumption. Failing to clean or replace air filters regularly can lead to engine damage.

5. **Neglecting Oil Changes:**
Skipping or delaying oil changes can cause engine components to wear out faster due to increased friction and heat. This can significantly shorten the engine's service life. Stay militant with keeping track of when you need to change the oil in your work vehicles and mowers.

6. **Disregarding Spark Plugs:**
Old or faulty spark plugs can lead to starting difficulties, engine misfires, and poor fuel economy. Regular checks and replacements are necessary for optimal performance. As I mentioned earlier, take advantage of rain days. It can be a great time to swap out air filters, change your spark plugs, bulk sharpen your blades, etc...

7. **Improper Storage:**
Storing equipment with fuel in the tank (especially over winter) without adding a stabilizer can lead to fuel degradation, which may clog the carburetor. Also, exposing equipment to the elements without proper coverage can accelerate wear and tear.

8. **Ignoring Tire Pressure:**
For equipment with tires, neglecting tire pressure checks can lead to uneven cuts and increased wear on the equipment. It also makes the equipment harder to maneuver. There are more and more options to purchase "flat-free tires" or "no-flat tires" for lawn mowers. These tires are

designed to never go flat because they are made from solid rubber or filled with a polyurethane foam, offering the durability needed for lawn care without the maintenance or hassle of pneumatic tires. Talk to your dealer and find out if these are a good fit for your lawn mowers, but in most cases making this switch could save you in the long run.

9. **Using the Wrong Fuel or Oil:**
Using incorrect fuel or oil types can damage the engine. For example, using fuel with too high ethanol content in machines not designed for it can cause damage. Or in the example I shared earlier pouring straight gas into a Stihl BR600 backpack blower will send that blower to the graveyard. Be intentional to train your team the proper procedures of what fuel and oil you use and why.

10. **DIY Repairs Without Proper Knowledge:**
Diving into DIY repairs on complex machinery without the necessary expertise or tools can exacerbate issues, risking further damage and possibly invalidating warranties. While conducting in-house repairs can be cost-effective for those with the mechanical know-how, maintaining a solid relationship with a skilled mechanic is invaluable. In markets like Atlanta, where major lawn mower repair shops face lengthy wait times, having access to a dependable mechanic who can offer quick turnaround times is crucial. Should you manage to secure a proficient mechanic, it's essential to ensure their satisfaction and availability for your future repair needs, as this could significantly streamline your operations and minimize downtime.

Avoiding these mistakes requires a commitment to regular maintenance schedules, a willingness to invest time in proper care, and the knowledge to recognize when professional help is needed. This not only prolongs the life of the equipment but also ensures it operates at peak efficiency, saving time and money in the long run. Just like top athletes take care of their bodies to perform at their best, if we want to be the best in our businesses we need to make sure our tools are in great shape.

Using Computers and Phones to Help

There are so many cool tools on computers and phones that can make running your lawn care business feel like playing a game.

- **Managing Customers:** There are programs that help you keep track of all your jobs, what your customers want, and when you need to go to their house next. I would recommend every lawn care business use a CRM. As I often mention on the Green Industry Podcast, I have used Jobber since 2019. It's ideal for lawn care businesses and they have a special offer for you at getjobber.com/paul

- **Talking to Customers:** Use email or messages to remind your customers when you're coming or to say thank you. You can even use social media to show off your great work. Where people's attention is online is ever changing, but at the time of writing this book I would certainly have fresh pictures of your work on your Google Business Profile, Instagram and Facebook.

- **Handling Money:** Programs like QuickBooks Online make dealing with money easier. You can see how much you're making, pay your friends who help, and even save some money for when you need new tools or have to fix something.

The reason I like Quickbooks Online is that it easily syncs with Jobber and it's the one my bookkeepers, Megan and Joey Coberly from the Landscaping Bookkeeper recommend. I do my invoicing through Jobber and all my accounting through Quickbooks Online and it works great for my customers, my bookkeepers and my business.

Conclusion: Making Your Business Run Smoothly

Making your lawn care business run smoothly is all about finding shortcuts and using tools that help you work better, not harder. By planning your routes, scheduling smartly, taking care of your tools, and using technology, you can make your business just like a well-played game: fun, efficient, and winning.

Remember, the goal is to make your work a little easier every day. By following these tips, you can have more time to enjoy your work, make your customers happy, and grow your business into something awesome.

CHAPTER 11

BUILDING A WINNING CULTURE IN YOUR LAWN CARE BUSINESS

WHEN PEOPLE ASK ME HOW TO find great workers for their lawn care business, I usually ask back, "Would you want to work for your own company?" I wait a bit to let them think. Most of the time, if they're really honest, they say, "No." Then, I tell them if we want really good people to work for us, like the best workers or companies we might hire to help, we need to make our company a place they'd love to be a part of. In this chapter, we're going to talk about how to make our lawn care business really awesome—a place where everyone wants to work. Let's be real, sometimes working inside where it's cool and comfy might seem nicer than working outside cutting grass, moving mulch, laying down grass squares, and being out in the hot sun or cold air. But, I know some lawn and garden businesses that are really special places to work. My friend Marvin Salcido talked about how to make a great place to work at a big meeting called the LCR Summit, and this chapter is a lot about what he said. These are the things I learned and thought were most important from his talk. If you're listening to this as an audiobook, we put in an extra special chapter at the end where you can hear Marvin's talk about making a great place to work. But right here, I'm going to tell you my top lessons on how to make your lawn care business a place where the best people want to work.

My Takeaways from Mavin's Salcido Speech on Company Culture at the LCR Summit:

1. Company Culture is Like a Garden: Marvin Salcido shared an enlightening perspective on company culture, comparing it to the soil in a garden. This analogy beautifully illustrates the idea that for a business to thrive and grow, the foundation—or culture—must be nurtured and healthy. Just as plants need fertile soil to bloom, a business requires a positive, supportive environment to flourish. Cultivating such a culture means fostering a space where employees feel valued, motivated, and connected to the company's goals.

2. Time and Attention: In his speech, Marvin highlighted the importance of managing time effectively, much like deciding how to spend a lunch break wisely. This metaphor extends to how business owners should invest time in their employees. Giving time and attention to your team is crucial, as it can significantly impact the business's productivity and morale. It's about prioritizing your team's needs and showing them that their contributions are valued, which in turn, strengthens the company culture.

3. Warning Signs are Opportunities: Marvin shares a cool idea about looking out for early signs that something might be going wrong in our lawn care work, kind of like when you notice dark clouds before a rainstorm. If we see something small that's not quite right, like maybe our lawn mower isn't cutting grass as well as it should, it's a hint that we need to do something about it. It's like being a detective, finding clues, and solving the problem before it turns into a bigger issue. This way, we keep our business running well and our team happy.

4. "Think Big, Stay Small": Embracing the "Think Big, Stay Small" philosophy means setting ambitious goals while maintaining the efficiency and agility of a smaller operation. Marvin emphasized the importance of planning for the future with a big vision in mind, yet also staying grounded in the practicalities of day-to-day operations. This approach ensures that the business can scale and grow without losing the qualities that make it unique and successful.

5. Branding and Love for the Job: Marvin's passion for his brand and his work is infectious. He believes that showing love for what you do and the brand you represent can inspire your team to take pride in their work. This sense of pride and ownership is contagious, leading to a team that's more engaged, motivated, and committed to the company's success. Branding isn't just about logos and marketing; it's about embodying the values and passion behind the business.

6. Valuing People Over Tasks: One of the key messages from Marvin was the importance of seeing employees as humans first, rather than just workers completing tasks. Understanding and acknowledging their personal lives, challenges, and achievements creates a culture of empathy and respect. This human-centric approach fosters loyalty and dedication among team members, making them feel valued and understood.

7. Continuous Learning and Preparation: Even before hiring his first employee, Marvin was keen on learning about payroll, hiring, and other essential business processes. This level of preparation and commitment to continuous learning ensured a smoother transition as his business expanded. It's a testament to the idea that being well-prepared and informed can significantly reduce the challenges of growth and change.

8. Celebrating Individual Contributions: Acknowledging and celebrating the efforts and achievements of each team member can have a profound impact on company culture. Marvin stresses the importance of recognizing individual contributions, which reinforces the value of every employee's work. Celebrating successes, big or small, boosts morale and encourages a culture of appreciation and recognition.

9. The Power of Apology: Marvin highlighted the strength in being able to admit mistakes and apologize when necessary. This approach builds respect and trust within the team, as it shows leadership vulnerability and accountability. An apology can go a long way in mending misunderstandings and reinforcing a culture of openness and honesty.

10. Open Communication: Encouraging team members to share their ideas and concerns freely is crucial for innovation and problem-solving. Marvin's emphasis on open communication channels fosters an environment where employees feel safe and valued in expressing their thoughts. This openness leads to a more collaborative and innovative workplace, where everyone feels part of the company's success.

11. Work-Life Balance: Marvin advocates for respecting personal time and encouraging a healthy balance between work and life. By scheduling work in a way that respects employees' need for personal time, the company shows that it values their well-being. This balance leads to happier, more productive employees who are less likely to experience burnout.

12. Investing in Team Growth: Offering training and opportunities for advancement demonstrates a commitment to employee development. Marvin's willingness to invest in his team's growth not only enhances their skills but also their loyalty to the company. Supporting employees in their career paths shows that the company is invested in their long-term success, both personally and professionally.

13. Handling Difficult Situations with Grace: Navigating challenges and making tough decisions with care and respect is vital. Marvin's approach to addressing performance issues or business changes emphasizes the importance of handling these situations gracefully. Treating employees with respect, even if it is difficult.

14. Celebrate Team Successes Together: A really good way to make everyone feel like they are part of the team is to celebrate when the team does something great. This means if your lawn care business finishes a big project or gets a compliment from a happy customer, you should have a little party or do something fun as a team. This shows everyone that their hard work is noticed and that they are an important part of the team. It's like when you win a game or do really well on a test at school, and your family or teacher is proud of you. It makes you feel good and want to do even better next time.

Conclusion

Building a winning culture in your lawn care business isn't just about cutting grass or making gardens look nice. It's about making a place where everyone feels happy to come to work, where they feel like they are part of a family, and where they know they are doing something important. From listening to Marvin Salcido and thinking about how to make a great workplace, we learned that we need to care about each other, work together well, and always try to do our best. Remember, a happy team will make your customers happy too, and that's what makes your business really special. So, let's make our lawn care business a place where the best people want to work, by being kind, working hard, and celebrating our wins together.

CHAPTER 12

LEARN TO EXCEL AT CUSTOMER SERVICE

I N THE COMPETITIVE ARENA OF LAWN care services and landscaping, customer service excellence is not just a value-added feature— it's a critical differentiator that sets your business apart from the amateurs. This chapter delves into the strategic importance of delivering outstanding customer service, a factor that not only retains customers but also transforms them into advocates for your brand, generating valuable referrals. For a lawn care business aiming for sustainability and growth, understanding and implementing superior customer service practices is akin to mastering a core business competency.

Understanding Customer Service in Lawn Care

Customer service in the lawn care industry transcends the mere execution of technical tasks; it encompasses the entire customer experience, from the initial contact to the post-service follow-up. It involves understanding customer needs, exceeding their expectations, and creating a lasting positive impression. Effective customer service is about building relationships and ensuring that every interaction adds value to the customer's perception of your brand.

The Importance of Customer Retention and Referrals

Customer retention is significantly more cost-effective than customer acquisition. Let me say that again in case you missed it, customer retention is significantly more cost-effective than customer acquisition. Satisfied customers provide a steady revenue stream and are more likely to purchase additional services. Moreover, they serve as organic brand ambassadors. Referrals from happy customers are a powerful marketing tool because they come with built-in trust and credibility. As we discussed in chapter 9 there is more to marketing a lawn care business than just customer referrals, but in my opinion and many others, customer referrals is a major key to building route density and attracting your ideal customers. In the lawn care business, where the quality of service directly impacts customer satisfaction, delivering exceptional customer service is the most effective strategy to harness the benefits of customer loyalty and word-of-mouth marketing.

Strategies for Delivering Outstanding Customer Service

Personalized Service: Tailor your services to meet the specific needs and preferences of your customers. Use customer data to remember important details such as service preferences, special requests, and even personal milestones. Personalization shows your commitment to their satisfaction.

In today's highly competitive lawn care industry, distinguishing your service isn't just about the quality of lawn maintenance you provide; it's also about the small, thoughtful gestures that exceed your customers' expectations. An excellent example of such a gesture is managing trash bins for your customers, especially on collection days.

Imagine this scenario: It's trash collection day, and after servicing a customer's property, you notice their empty trash bins left out by the curb. Instead of ignoring them, you take a moment to roll the bins back to their usual storage spot near the garage. This simple act of consideration saves your customer the hassle and demonstrates a level of care and attention to detail that goes well beyond the expected lawn maintenance services.

This gesture may seem minor in the grand scheme of things, but it's these small acts of kindness that leave a lasting impression on your customers. They show that you're observant, thoughtful, and willing to go the extra mile for their convenience. Such actions contribute significantly to building a positive relationship with your clients, fostering loyalty, and enhancing your business's reputation for outstanding customer service.

Furthermore, these considerate practices can serve as a powerful differentiator in a crowded market. When customers share their experiences with friends, family, or through online reviews, it's often these special touches that they highlight, acting as compelling testimonials to the quality and care your service provides.

Once upon a time one of my customers was the Defensive Coordinator of the Atlanta Falcons. They had a Monday Night Football game that evening in Tampa, Florida against the Tampa Bay Buccaneers. During the day, I was tending to the maintenance of this customer's stunning property. And I knew his wife was out of town, and of course I knew the football coach was out of town coaching in the big game. I also realized they forgot to take out their trash since they were both out of town. I knew their garage code because they trusted me and gave it to me so I could adjust their sprinkler system as needed throughout the year. And so what I did was I opened their garage and rolled out their full trash cans to the curb because I knew the trash collection company comes early Tuesday morning. This turned out to be a great idea, and earned me massive brownie points with the football coach/my customer.

Although the Falcons managed to win the game and the coach was in a good mood post-game. They had a long flight home and by the time my customer got home after the game it was actually 4:30 am. As he was approaching his home extremely tired he realized he was going to have to take the trash to the curb since his wife was out of town. But when he got home and pulled in the driveway he saw his trash cans already at the curb. Long story short he later reached out to me and asked if I had taken the initiative to take out his trash cans and I let him know that I did do that. He was very very happy and thankful. It honestly only took me 2 minutes, but the Coach was so pleased with me being proactive and aware about that situation. He ended up getting me tickets that year to the Falcons playoff game versus the Seattle Seahawks as well as the NFC Championship where they beat the Packers and went to the Super Bowl. It was epic, and in hindsight what got me favor with my influential customer was not just that I had their property looking pristine year round, but it was the small personalized touches showing them that I was intentional to go above and beyond to make sure their property and home was well managed.

In conclusion, excelling in customer service requires looking for opportunities to add value in unexpected ways. Rolling trash bins back after collection is just one example of how lawn care professionals can demonstrate their commitment to service excellence. It underscores the importance of being proactive, attentive, and considerate, reinforcing your company's reputation as not just a lawn care provider but as a thoughtful partner in maintaining their home's exterior.

Proactive Communication: Maintain open lines of communication with your customers. Proactively update them about service schedules, any potential changes, or recommendations for their lawn care. Transparency builds trust and demonstrates your professionalism. CRM's like Jobber make it easy to communicate to your customers. For example if there are weather related issues and you won't perform your services it's always a good idea to let the customer know early and often. They will appreciate that. And perhaps you are picking up on an idea I keep insinuating and that is being proactive. Whether it's being proactive in retrieving trash cans or proactive in communicating that because of the forecasted rain you will be arriving the next day, being intentional and proactive can set you apart from the competition.

Responsiveness to Feedback and Complaints: Transforming Challenges into Opportunities

In the realm of lawn care, responsiveness to feedback and complaints is not merely a procedural task—it's a strategic approach to enhancing service quality and fostering customer loyalty. Viewing feedback and complaints through the lens of opportunity allows for growth and improvement. A timely, thoughtful response to customer concerns can transform dissatisfaction into loyalty, and even advocacy.

This principle was vividly illustrated in a personal experience I've recounted on the Green Industry Podcast. Reflecting on it now, it's astonishing how a complaint became a pivotal networking and business growth opportunity. It was on a brisk Saturday morning, amidst the busiest part of my week, that this lesson unfolded. Saturdays were crucial for me that year, given my 29-hour workweek at the radio station. This tight schedule meant that Saturdays offered the most significant window to service my customers, working diligently from the moment the gates to Sugarloaf Country Club opened until my evening shift at the radio station.

Understanding the importance of respecting our clients' peace, especially in the early hours, my strategy involved scheduling services at homes that were often unoccupied first thing in the morning. One such property belonged to affluent clients who primarily resided in California, using their Atlanta residence as a second home for occasional golf retreats. Unbeknownst to me, this early morning routine had sparked frustration among the neighbors.

On one chilly Saturday, while running an errand, I received an unexpected call from Robert, my dependable laborer, known for his proactive and meticulous approach to work. Given Robert's self-sufficiency, his call signaled something out of the ordinary. Indeed, he was on the line with me, while an irate neighbor was confronting him about the disturbance caused by our early work. Quickly, I advised halting the noise and decided to address the situation personally.

Approaching the neighbor's door to offer a heartfelt apology for the oversight, I was met with a mix of surprise and appreciation. My explanation of our choice to service the usually vacant property first on Saturdays sparked a conversation that swiftly transitioned from tension to opportunity. The neighbor, impressed by a sod job we had completed nearby, invited me to meet her husband, the local football coach, and discuss their own lawn care needs over a warm cup of coffee.

This encounter not only resolved a complaint but also opened the door to a new client relationship with the Defensive Coordinator of the Atlanta Falcons. This connection blossomed into a fruitful network of referrals within the NFL community, transforming a moment of criticism into a life-changing business opportunity.

This story underscores the power of addressing feedback with humility and responsiveness. It highlights the potential for complaints to reveal opportunities not just for resolution but for remarkable growth and networking. The key lies in seeing beyond the immediate discomfort of criticism, approaching each interaction with sincerity, and being open to the unexpected paths and where they may lead us.

Not every challenge can be transformed into an opportunity. Some situations serve as stark reminders of the consequences of miscommunication and oversight. One such instance, involving Mrs. Wilson, a kindly widow, offers a poignant lesson in the importance of setting clear service boundaries, maintaining open communication with your team, and the potential repercussions of falling short in customer service.

During my "Survival Mode Steve" phase, my eagerness to accommodate any customer request led me to accept a job outside my usual scope of services. Mrs. Wilson requested we pressure wash her deck—a task that, while simple in nature, required careful attention to detail, especially regarding her specific instructions to remove and later replace all items from the deck. This job fell on Joe, a reliable team member, while I was attending to maintenance jobs in another location.

Joe executed the pressure washing with precision, restoring the deck to look as good as new. However, a crucial oversight occurred. Opting for caution, Joe decided against replacing the furniture immediately due to the wet conditions of the deck, intending to communicate this decision to me for later follow-up. Unfortunately, this critical piece of information was never relayed, leading to an oversight that would have significant repercussions.

Mrs. Wilson's reaction to the unfinished job was one of understandable frustration. Despite the quality of the work done on the deck, the failure to meet her full request led to a severing of our professional relationship. Worse still, her dissatisfaction did not remain confined to her experience alone; it rippled through the neighborhood, resulting in the loss of additional clients.

This incident underscored several vital lessons for me as a business owner. Firstly, the necessity of clear and concise service offerings cannot be overstated. Agreeing to tasks beyond your core services without proper planning and communication can lead to mishaps that jeopardize customer satisfaction and business reputation. Secondly, the importance of thorough communication within the team is paramount. A simple miscommunication between Joe and myself resulted in a cascade of negative consequences. Lastly, this experience highlighted the crucial role of leadership in ensuring that every job is followed through to completion, according to the customer's expectations.

From this challenging experience, I learned the value of implementing more structured communication protocols within my team and the significance of directly overseeing tasks that fall outside our standard service range. It was a harsh reminder that in the world of customer service, the devil is often in the details, and leadership involves not just delegating tasks but ensuring they are completed to the client's satisfaction. While not every complaint can lead to a positive outcome, each one offers an opportunity for reflection, learning, and improvement.

Consistency in Quality: Ensure that every service delivered meets a high standard of quality. Consistency is key to building customer trust and satisfaction. Implement quality control measures to maintain service excellence across all customer touchpoints. For example as I often share on my podcast if you are mowing, make sure you have sharp blades each morning. Back in the summer of 2018 I visited Bryan Ring in Minnesota and toured his operation for the day. It was great to see in the afternoon when the various crews rolled in back to the shop they immediately propped up the Toro lawn mowers and swapped out the blades with fresh blades. That way in the next morning they started the day with fresh razor sharp blades. It's great to have a plan of how you are going to keep your lawn mower blades sharp along with other equipment running at top performance.

Additionally, I would recommend finding a local mentor, who can teach you the proper way to do landscaping with quality. One of my mentors Kenny was well established in the Country Club of the South that featured remarkable properties. And so during my first couple years of starting my business, when Kenny needed a hand on his crews, I would work with them for the day. This taught me how to properly reel mow a lawn to make it look like a golf course, as well as how to properly prune a rose bush, and how to make the edges sharp and puffy on pine straw installs and so much more. My point is to quickly learn how to do quality work and then do it consistently.

Employee Development and Motivation: A Key to Customer Service Success

The personnel of your company aren't just employees; they're the ambassadors of your brand. Prioritizing their continuous development through structured training programs is crucial for elevating the standard of customer service your business is known for. Employees who are engaged and proficient in their roles are instrumental in creating positive customer experiences that lead to repeat business and high-quality referrals. To delve deeper into effective strategies for employee training and engagement, I recommend exploring my Green Industry Podcast YouTube channel. Here, you'll find insightful discussions with leaders of industry giants like Dave Fairburn's North Point Outdoors, Jonathan Pototschnik's CitiTurf, and Jeremy Talboy's North Georgia Landscape Management, each managing businesses with annual revenues exceeding $10 million. These in-depth videos offer a treasure trove of strategies for nurturing a motivated workforce committed to excellence. The underlying message from these leaders is clear: valuing your team, providing them with a clear growth trajectory within your organization, and fostering a work environment they're proud to be part of are foundational to achieving outstanding customer service.

Cultivating a Culture of Customer Service Excellence

Creating a culture that prioritizes customer service excellence begins with leadership. Set clear expectations for service standards and lead by example. Celebrate instances of exceptional customer service within your team to reinforce its value. Encourage employees to take initiative in creating positive customer experiences and empower them to make decisions that enhance customer satisfaction.

Measuring Success and Continuous Improvement

Regularly measure customer satisfaction through surveys, feedback forms, and direct communication. Analyze this data to identify trends, areas for improvement, and opportunities to innovate your service offering. Continuous improvement in customer service should be a core objective of your business strategy.

Conclusion

In the landscape of lawn care services, where differentiation is often challenging, customer service excellence emerges as a potent strategic advantage. It not only secures customer loyalty and retention but also catalyzes word-of-mouth referrals, driving business growth. By embedding customer service excellence into your business DNA, you establish a foundation for sustainable success. Remember, in the competitive field of lawn care, the quality of your customer service is as visible as the lawns you maintain—it reflects the health and vibrancy of your business.

CHAPTER 13

UNDERSTANDING THE LIFETIME VALUE OF A LAWN CARE CUSTOMER

ONE DEFINING TRAIT OF SUCCESSFUL INDIVIDUALS is their ability to think long-term. Rather than merely focusing on immediate or short-term results, they evaluate how their choices will impact their futures over spans of five, ten years, or even more. In this chapter, we delve into the concept of Customer Lifetime Value (LTV) within the realm of the lawn care industry. Grasping the significance of LTV is vital, as it greatly shapes strategies for business growth, profitability, and effective customer relationship management, setting a foundation for sustained success. If you are at the onset of your lawn care business venture, envisioning a decade ahead might seem daunting. However, I can personally attest to the speed at which time flies and relationships solidify; one of my initial clients, the respected Dr. Kim remained with my business for over ten years. In this chapter, we not only explore the theoretical underpinnings of LTV but also illustrate how these concepts manifest in real-world scenarios, affirming the swift passage of time in building enduring business relationships. Before we delve into the intricacies of LTV, it's imperative to emphasize that long-term customer retention hinges on consistently delivering **quality service**. Assuming you are providing top-notch service, let us examine the profound implications of understanding LTV in depth

Understanding Lifetime Value (LTV)

The Lifetime Value of a customer is a crucial metric that represents the total revenue a business can reasonably expect from a single customer account throughout their relationship with the company. For lawn care businesses, where services are typically recurring, understanding LTV is vital for making informed decisions regarding customer acquisition, retention, and service offerings.

Significance of LTV in Lawn Care

Guided Business Decisions: LTV provides a clear picture of what a customer is worth over time, helping businesses allocate marketing and operational resources more effectively.

Enhanced Customer Retention: Knowing the long-term value of customers can justify the investments made in loyalty programs and retention strategies, which are often less costly than acquiring new customers.

Service Optimization: By understanding the revenue potential of different customer segments, lawn care businesses can tailor their services to maximize satisfaction and profitability for high-value customers.

Financial Planning: LTV assists in financial forecasting and planning, allowing businesses to predict cash flow and profit margins more accurately.

Calculating LTV: A Detailed Example

To illustrate the concept of LTV, consider a lawn care business that offers multiple recurring services to its customers. We'll calculate the LTV of a typical customer over a 10-year period, factoring in annual price increases and the addition of services.

- **Initial Setup:** A customer subscribes to a monthly lawn maintenance program at $400. Additionally, they opt for yearly core aeration at $250 and mulch installation at $1500 annually. These are very common services in the south. Customers want year round services that include fertilizer and weed control and they want a core aeration once a year as well as their mulch or pine straw freshened up each season.

- **Annual Price Increase:** Prices for all services increase by 5% each year to keep up with inflation and rising operational costs. I chose 5% for the sake of this example, but the average is to raise your rates at least 5-10% annually, although I know some local companies that raise their rates even more than that.

Projected Revenue Calculation

Using the initial data and projecting a 5% annual increase, we can calculate the expected revenue from this customer over 10 years:

- **Monthly Maintenance:** Starts at $400/month and increases annually. The total over 10 years, with a compounding increase, is approximately $62,000.

- **Core Aeration Service:** At an initial $250 with a 5% yearly increase, the total over 10 years is around $3,300.

- **Mulch Installation:** Starting at $1500 with the same annual increase, amounts to about $25,000 over the decade.

Total LTV for this customer over 10 years is estimated at $90,300.

Strategies to Enhance LTV in Your Business

Commitment to Quality: Consistently delivering high-quality services ensures customer satisfaction, fostering loyalty and reducing churn.

Personalized Communication: Regular, personalized contact with customers helps maintain a connection and makes them feel valued, which is crucial for retention.

Customer Feedback Loop: Regularly solicit feedback and quickly address any concerns or complaints. This not only improves service quality but also demonstrates your commitment to customer satisfaction, which can convert average customers into loyal clients.

Effective Upselling and Cross-Selling: Introducing customers to additional services can enhance their overall satisfaction and increase the revenue generated per customer. The example I shared was very conservative just including the weekly maintenance along with a core aeration and yearly mulch install, but there are so many other services to upsell and cross sell such as:

- **Landscape Design** - Offering design services for garden and landscape improvements.
- **Tree and Shrub Care** - Providing pruning, fertilization, and disease prevention for trees and shrubs.
- **Gutter Cleaning** - Adding gutter cleaning services, especially in fall.
- **Pressure Washing** - Offering pressure washing for driveways, sidewalks, and patios.
- **Leaf Removal** - Providing leaf removal services in the autumn.
- **Seasonal Clean-Up** - Offering spring and fall clean-up services to prepare gardens and yards for the coming season.

- **Sod Installation** - Laying new sod for instant lawn improvement.
- **Landscape Lighting** - Installing or maintaining outdoor lighting systems.
- **Water Features** - Installing or maintaining ponds, fountains, and waterfalls. Check out my friend Greg Wittstock "The Pond Guy" for recommendations on these services.
- **Irrigation Systems** - Installing new irrigation systems or maintaining and repairing existing systems.
- **Planting Services** - Planting annuals, perennials, shrubs, or trees to enhance landscape aesthetics.
- **Hardscaping** - Offering services like patio, walkway, or retaining wall construction.
- **Snow Removal** - Providing snow plowing and salting services in the winter months. If you listen to me on the Green Industry Podcast you know I like the warm weather lol, but hey plow that snow and make that dough!
- **Holiday Decor** - Offering seasonal decoration services for holidays, especially Christmas lighting and decor, just don't be like Clark Grizwald in Christmas Vacation.

Now, even if you offer just a few of those upsells, you could easily pass the $100,000 revenue of LTV per customer.

Conclusion

In conclusion, the LTV of a customer is a fundamental measure that every lawn care business should understand and utilize in its strategic planning. By focusing on maximizing the LTV of each customer, businesses can enhance their operational efficiency, boost profitability, and secure a stable, growing customer base. This strategic focus ensures that the business not only survives but thrives in the competitive landscape of lawn care services.

CHAPTER 14

THE POWER OF PUNCTUALITY

PUNCTUALITY GOES BEYOND MERE TIMELINESS; IT embodies respect, reliability, and professionalism. It shows that you value other people's time as much as your own. In the competitive lawn care industry, where reliability can distinguish your business from others, being punctual can significantly impact your business's success and reputation.

"Punctuality is the soul of business."
– THOMAS C. HALIBURTON

This quote encapsulates the vital role that punctuality plays in any business, especially in service industries like lawn care. Being punctual is not merely a courtesy; it's a cornerstone of business ethics and a fundamental aspect of your brand's integrity and reputation.

Why Punctuality Matters in Lawn Care

Imagine you have a scheduled tee time at Augusta National Golf Club—a place of impeccable beauty and tradition, where legends like Tiger Woods have crafted some of the most memorable moments in golf history. If invited by Tiger himself, you wouldn't dare be late, would you? This analogy extends directly to how you should approach every client interaction in your lawn care business. Just as you would arrive early, prepared, and ready to seize a once-in-a-lifetime golfing opportunity, so too should you approach each customer appointment with the same level of enthusiasm and commitment.

Being on time in the lawn care business means showing up as promised, ready to work, and prepared for the day's tasks. It's a visible measure of your respect for clients' time and a direct reflection of your company's reliability.

Punctuality and Its Impact on Business

Builds Trust: When you are consistently on time, clients trust you more. Trust leads to longer relationships, which we discussed under Customer Lifetime Value in the previous chapter. If there is a weather delay, be proactive and communicate clearly with your customers when your team will be there.

Enhances Reputation: In an industry rife with complaints about reliability, being punctual sets you apart as a dependable provider, enhancing your reputation and increasing referrals.

Reduces Stress: For both you and your client, punctuality means that scheduled work proceeds as planned, reducing stress and allowing for better execution of service.

Improves Team Morale: When the leader emphasizes punctuality, it sets the tone for the entire team, leading to improved efficiency and morale.

Implementing Punctuality in Your Business

To integrate punctuality into your lawn care business, consider the following strategies:

- **Scheduling Software:** Use scheduling software to keep track of appointments, send reminders to clients and staff, and adjust schedules promptly to handle any unforeseen delays. I recommend Jobber and you can get a discount when you sign up for Jobber at thePaulJamison.com

- **Buffer Times:** Always schedule buffer times between jobs to accommodate unexpected delays like traffic or extended service times at a previous job. Until you really get dialed in, most jobs typically take a little longer than you initially expect.

- **Communication:** Maintain clear communication with clients and team members. If a delay is unavoidable, inform all affected parties as soon as possible. I mentioned this earlier in this chapter and often on the Green Industry Podcast because it is very important to customer retention. Communicate well!

- **Employee Training:** Train your team on the importance of punctuality and how their timeliness impacts the business and its reputation.

- **Lead by Example:** As the business owner, set a punctual example. Arrive early, start meetings on time, and respect your team's time.

Quotes to Inspire Punctuality

"I could never think well of a man's intellectual or moral character if he was habitually unfaithful to his appointments."
– NATHANIEL EMMONS

"Punctuality is one of the cardinal business virtues: always insist on it in your subordinates."
— DON MARQUIS

"Being on time to appointments and meetings is a phase of self-discipline and an evidence of self-respect. Punctuality is a courteous compliment the intelligent person pays to his associates."
— MARVIN J. ASHTON

Conclusion

In the lawn care business, punctuality is more than a preference—it is a practice. It shows that you value your clients' time and are serious about the service you provide. It builds lasting relationships based on trust and mutual respect. By fostering a culture of punctuality within your team, you are setting your business up for long-term success and establishing a reputation as a reliable, professional service provider. Let's make every minute count, for in the lawn care industry, every minute truly matters.

CHAPTER 15

THE PROSPEROUS MINDSET

I N MY JOURNEY OF ENTREPRENEURSHIP, ONE of the most transformative experiences occurred not out in the field, but within the confines of my own mind. A shift in mindset from scarcity to abundance has not only impacted my actions and behaviors but has been the catalyst for substantial growth in both my business revenue and personal income. I have been replacing some "bad" thoughts that I had about business and money with "good" thoughts and those improved thoughts have therefore influenced my actions which have helped accelerate wealth creation.

Influences on My Prosperous Mindset

The development of my prosperous mindset owes much to the teachings of Dave Ramsey, Daniel Lapin, and Myron Golden. Each has contributed uniquely to my understanding of wealth. Their insights have helped refine my approach to not just earning but multiplying wealth, a principle that any successful entrepreneur will affirm: your income should generate assets, and those assets should, in turn, generate further income.

Dave Ramsey and the Foundations of Financial Peace

My introduction to Dave Ramsey's principles began at his Total Money Makeover Event in Duluth, GA, in 2010. Ramsey's approach, which focuses on eliminating debt and building wealth systematically, was an eye-opener. His "baby steps," which advocate for building an emergency fund, paying off all debt via the "debt snowball" method, and then investing wisely, laid the groundwork for financial freedom. Ramsey's emphasis on "gazelle intensity" and focus — much like the gazelle that outruns a faster cheetah by sheer necessity — underscored the urgency of financial prudence and the power of directed effort.

Myron Golden's Millionaire Mindset

Myron Golden's teachings delve into the psychological transformations necessary to achieve and sustain wealth. His concept of the "Millionaire Mindset" is not merely about harboring a desire to be wealthy but igniting a "burning desire" to achieve financial goals. Golden stresses the importance of converting desire into action, advocating for rapid wealth accumulation not through shortcuts, but through diligent, value-driven work. His strategies include minimizing distractions like television until financial goals are met, focusing on solutions that serve customers well, and leveraging one's capabilities to their fullest potential.

Daniel Lapin's Insights into Prosperity

Daniel Lapin's book, "Thou Shall Prosper," provides a profound understanding of why certain communities have historically excelled at wealth creation. Lapin argues that viewing money as a certificate of performance, awarded when one successfully serves another, transforms the pursuit of wealth from a selfish endeavor to a community-enhancing activity. This perspective aligns with biblical teachings that not only endorse prosperity but depict it as a divine reward for stewardship and service.

Building a Prosperous Mindset

Commit to Education and Continuous Learning: The gap between where you are and where you want to be is filled with the knowledge you acquire and apply. Invest in learning and mentorship. I've personally attended live events hosted by both Dave Ramsey and Myron Golden.

Focus on Value Creation: Like Ramsey and Golden suggest, wealth is generated more swiftly and sustainably when focusing on providing value and solving problems for others.

Manage Wealth Wisely: Following Ramsey's advice, using your income judiciously to clear debt and then to invest wisely sets the foundation for long-term financial security.

Adopt a Service Mindset: As Lapin highlights, prosperity flows from a mindset of service. When your business solves real problems, financial rewards naturally follow.

Embrace Community and Network Building: Wealth creation is not a solitary journey. Engaging with like-minded individuals can accelerate your growth and open new avenues for creating wealth.

Conclusion

The journey from a scarcity mindset to one of abundance and prosperity is challenging but deeply rewarding. It's about more than just financial gain—it's about cultivating a life enriched with purpose and the power to positively impact those around you. Through the teachings of mentors like Ramsey, Golden, and Lapin, I've not only reshaped my approach to business and wealth but have also discovered the profound joy in serving others and watching the community thrive alongside me.

CHAPTER 16

LEARNING FROM MISTAKES— A PATHWAY TO MASTERY

EVERY ENTREPRENEUR'S JOURNEY IS PUNCTUATED BY setbacks and failures, but the true measure of success is not in avoiding mistakes, but in harnessing them as stepping stones towards greater achievements. In the lawn care business, where every new day brings its own set of challenges, learning from mistakes is not just a recommendation—it's a necessity.

The Philosophy of Mistakes

> *"Mistakes have the power to turn you into something better than you were before."*
> — Unknown

Embracing mistakes as opportunities for growth transforms the way we approach challenges in our business. It's essential to develop a mindset that views mistakes not as embarrassments or failures, but as vital lessons that pave the road to future success.

Common Mistakes in Lawn Care Business

Underpricing Services: Many new business owners, eager to attract clients, set their prices too low. This undermines the value of their service and can lead to financial strain. Correcting this involves understanding your costs, the value you provide, and researching competitive pricing.

Overpromising and Under-Delivering: It's easy to fall into the trap of promising too much in an effort to please clients. This often leads to customer dissatisfaction. Always ensure that what you promise can be realistically delivered.

Neglecting Equipment Maintenance: Failing to maintain equipment can lead to costly repairs and downtime. Implementing a regular maintenance schedule ensures reliability and efficiency.

Poor Hiring Decisions: Hiring in haste can lead to regret. Take time to thoroughly vet candidates to ensure they fit both the job requirements and your company culture.

Inadequate Customer Communication: Miscommunications with clients can lead to unmet expectations and lost business. Develop clear communication protocols to keep clients informed and engaged.

Turning Mistakes into Teachable Moments

The essence of learning from mistakes lies in turning them into teachable moments. Here's how to ensure that each mistake made becomes a building block for improvement:

- **Reflect on the Mistake:** Understand what went wrong and why. Reflecting helps prevent the recurrence of the same error.

- **Document the Lessons Learned:** Keep a record of mistakes and the insights they provided. This can become a valuable resource for training new team members.

- **Share Knowledge:** Encourage a culture where sharing mistakes is seen as a strength. This can lead to collective improvement and prevent others from making the same errors.

- **Adjust Processes:** Use the lessons learned to refine your business processes. This might mean updating training methods, improving client communication strategies, or enhancing quality control measures.

- **Forgive Yourself:** Recognize that making mistakes is a part of growth. Treat them as necessary steps in your learning curve.

Examples of Learning from Mistakes in Lawn Care

- A new lawn care owner once forgot to check the weather forecast and scheduled a major sod installation. A sudden downpour ruined hours of work. Now, weather checks are a standard part of his planning process, demonstrating the importance of adapting to environmental factors.

- Another common error is overbooking services without leaving time for unforeseen delays. One business owner learned to build buffer times into schedules after several instances of running late caused customer dissatisfaction.

Quotes to Inspire Recovery from Mistakes

"Do not be embarrassed by your failures, learn from them and start again."
— RICHARD BRANSON

"A person who never made a mistake never tried anything new."

— Albert Einstein

Conclusion

In the lawn care business, as in any other, the path to success is strewn with obstacles. Each mistake you encounter is a chance to refine your methods, enhance your business acumen, and elevate your service. By fostering a culture that views mistakes as opportunities for learning, you not only improve your operations but also enhance your team's resilience and adaptability. Remember, the goal is not to never make a mistake but to never make the same mistake twice. Let each error teach you something profound and lead you one step closer to mastering the art of lawn care.

CHAPTER 17

CULTIVATING CONNECTIONS FOR GROWTH

SUCCESS IN BUSINESS AND PERSONAL LIFE is significantly influenced by the people and environments we choose to surround ourselves with. In the lawn care industry, the strategic choice of location, customers, and associates plays a pivotal role in determining the trajectory of your business's growth. This chapter delves into the importance of making thoughtful connections, disengaging from detrimental associations, and positioning oneself in environments that foster success.

The Power of the Right Connections

> *"Surround yourself with people who push you to be your best self."*
> — UNKNOWN

The right connections can serve as catalysts for personal and professional growth. They can provide new insights, introduce you to valuable networks, and challenge you to excel beyond your perceived limits. Conversely, connections that drain your energy or detract from your values can hinder your progress.

Choosing the Right Geographical Location

Choosing the right geographical location is as crucial as selecting the right people. For a lawn care business, operating in neighborhoods that value and can afford premium services ensures the sustainability and profitability of your operations. Being in the right place not only increases the visibility of your business but also enhances the likelihood of acquiring clients who appreciate quality and are willing to pay for it.

Disconnecting from Negative Influences

"The less you respond to negative people, the more positive your life will become."
— PAULO COELHO

Separating from those who hold you back is not just about cutting ties; it's about making room for growth. This applies to inefficient business practices, underperforming team members, and personal relationships that do not support your vision. Recognizing the impact of negative influences and taking decisive action to reduce their presence can dramatically improve your focus and productivity.

Connecting with Uplifting Individuals

Engage with individuals who inspire integrity, accountability, and success. These relationships should encourage you to pursue excellence relentlessly. In business, this means working with those who not only share your vision but are also committed to ethical practices and excellence.

Building the Right Team

Your team is your biggest asset. Hiring individuals who are not only skilled but also align with your company's culture and values is crucial. They are the frontline representatives of your business and play a significant role in how your services are perceived by clients.

Networking Strategically

Effective networking transcends mere accumulation of contacts; it's fundamentally about forging relationships that offer mutual benefits. To maximize the potential of these relationships, it's crucial to be proactive in attending industry conferences, participating in community events, and engaging on online platforms. These venues serve as excellent opportunities to connect with potential mentors, peers, and customers who can contribute to your professional growth and business expansion. Notably, I regularly attend key industry gatherings such as the Equip Exposition held annually in October in Louisville, Kentucky, and Jason Creel's Lawn Care Life Conference in Springville, Alabama every February. For more details about these events, visit my website at thePaulJamison.com.

Maximizing Opportunities Through Strategic Placement and Timing

The significance of being strategically positioned at the opportune moment cannot be overstated. Success often hinges on the ability to be in the right place at the right time, which requires careful planning and a proactive stance in business. This involves positioning yourself where potential clients are most likely to seek your services and being adequately prepared to meet their demands as they arise. To align my daily actions with these opportunities, I begin each day with a focused intention, praying, "God, please guide me today to be in the right place, at the right time, doing the right things." This prayer not only sets the tone for my day but also underscores the importance of aligning my actions with strategic goals and timing.

Embracing Community Involvement

Engaging with the community not only builds goodwill but also establishes your business as a reliable and integral part of the neighborhood. This involvement can lead to referrals and a loyal customer base.

Personal Growth and Accountability

Surround yourself with people who hold you accountable for your actions and decisions. Personal growth is a continuous process, and having a support system that challenges you to stay true to your values and goals is invaluable.

Conclusion

In conclusion, separating from detrimental influences and cultivating the right connections are crucial for personal and business success. By positioning yourself in the right locations, surrounding yourself with the right people, and fostering a culture of excellence and accountability, you set the stage for sustained growth and success. Your network can be your greatest asset—choose it wisely, nurture it, and watch as it propels you towards your goals.

CHAPTER 18

EMPOWERING YOUR PATH TO SUCCESS

AS WE CLOSE THIS TRANSFORMATIVE JOURNEY through the landscapes of lawn care and personal growth, let's take a moment to reflect on what we've explored and how you can leverage these insights to truly excel in your business endeavors. This book has been crafted not merely as a guide but as a companion in your quest for excellence, whether you're trimming the edges of a small yard or sculpting the vast greens of expansive estates.

A Recap of Our Journey

From the foundational aspects of customer service excellence in Chapter 1 to the strategic business positioning discussed in Chapter 17, we have traversed a variety of topics vital for any entrepreneur eager to make a mark in the lawn care industry. We delved into the practicality of lawn care operations, the nuances of customer relationship management, the critical importance of punctuality, and the profound impact of adopting a prosperous mindset.

Cultivating Your Lawn Care Empire

Remember, the seeds of success in lawn care or any business lie in consistency, quality, and customer interaction. Every lawn mowed, every leaf blown, every piece of sod laid and every client interaction is a step towards building a reputation as reliable and dedicated service providers. Your commitment to excellence should be evident in every blade of grass you mow and every smile you foster through exceptional service.

Crush It in Your Business

To truly "crush it" in your business, embrace each challenge as an opportunity to learn and expand your skills. Maintain your curiosity, adapt to new circumstances, and continuously seek improvements. While the stories and strategies in this book provide a solid foundation, it's crucial to trust your instincts and innovate according to your unique business landscape. Remember, the business environment, much like the seasons, is always changing—what succeeded yesterday might not suffice tomorrow. Be ready to pivot and persevere. For ongoing insights and to stay current with industry best practices, tune into my podcast, the Green Industry Podcast.

Connect for Continued Growth

To ensure you are never alone on this journey, I also invite you to visit my website, thepauljamison.com, where you can find a wealth of resources to further your education and inspiration. Whether you're looking for the latest in lawn care innovations or seeking a community of like-minded entrepreneurs, it's all there waiting to help you push your boundaries and expand your capabilities.

Your Call to Action

As you turn the final page of this book, see it not as an end but as the onset of your entrepreneurial journey. With the insights and strategies you've gathered, you are poised to elevate your business to unparalleled levels of success. Remember, the excellence of your service and the integrity with which you operate will set you apart in any industry.

Step forward with confidence and enthusiasm, prepared to tackle the future. Greet each day with optimism, a solid plan, and a steadfast commitment to delivering outstanding service to your customers. Now is your moment to shine, turning every challenge into a golden opportunity. Let's make it happen—let's achieve greatness!

MORE RESOURCES
FROM PAUL JAMISON

Elevate your lawn care business with our exclusive "Know Your Numbers Course." Master crucial financial skills like calculating break-even rates, pricing for profitability, and effective billing strategies. Gain insights into managing cash flow and owner's compensation. This essential on-demand course is your gateway to financial success. Special Offer:

Enjoy 25% OFF—only available here!

PRICE INCREASE LETTER TEMPLATE

Enhance client communication with our Price Increase Letter Template, tailored for lawn care businesses. This ready-to-use template helps you professionally notify clients about rate changes, maintaining transparency and trust. It includes customizable sections for personal details and updated pricing, ensuring clear communication of necessary adjustments due to rising service costs. Secure ongoing relationships while managing financial changes effectively.

Special Offer: Get 25% OFF the Price Increase Letter Template—only available here!

SCAN ME

Made in the USA
Monee, IL
12 October 2024

67070027R00081